# TRANSLATING THE CLASSICS OF JUDAISM
## In Theory and In Practice

Number 176

# TRANSLATING THE CLASSICS OF JUDAISM
## In Theory and In Practice

by
Jacob Neusner

# TRANSLATING THE CLASSICS OF JUDAISM
## In Theory and In Practice



by
Jacob Neusner

Scholars Press
Atlanta, Georgia

# TRANSLATING THE CLASSICS OF JUDAISM
## In Theory and In Practice



**Library of Congress Cataloging in Publication Data**

Neusner, Jacob, 1932-
Translating the classics of Judaism : in theory and in practice / by Jacob Neusner.
p. cm. -- (Brown Judaic studies : no. 176)
Includes bibliographical references and index.
ISBN 1-55540-353-0 (alk. paper)
1. Rabbinical literature--Translations into English--History and criticism. 2. Talmud--Translating. 3. Rabbinical literature--Translating. I. Title. II. Series.
BM496.5.N4826 1989
296.1'205--dc20 89-6281
CIP

Printed in the United States of America
on acid-free paper

For

MAURICE-RUBEN HAYOUN

AND HIS WIFE CATHERINE

IN PARIS

ON THE OCCASION OF THEIR MARRIAGE

WITH THE LOVE OF THEIR AMERICAN FRIENDS

AND ADMIRERS IN PROVIDENCE

# Table of Contents

# Preface

I now near the end of nearly two decades of sustained work in translating into American English all of the classical documents of Judaism in its formative age, from the Mishnah through the Bavli or Babylonian Talmud, that is, ca. A.D. 200-600. I began with the Mishnah and Tosefta in 1972. By 1992 I shall have completed translating the final documents of the canon of the Judaism of the Dual Torah as scholarship assigns dates to the ancient writings. These translations of mine moreover have served as the foundation to introductions to each of these same documents, some of them quite ambitious. In all cases I mean to define the document that has been translated. So in all, I have worked my way through the whole of the canon of Judaism.[1] It is time to explain the theory of this work of translation and introduction, and that is my purpose in these essays.

I do so in three ways. First of all, I spell out the principles that I think must guide the work. Second, I compare my work with prior translations of the same documents by others in this century. Third, I spell out what I think is at stake in the mode of translating that I have invented for this literature, which I call "the analytical translation." In Chapters One, Eight, and Nine and Ten I present the theory of the matter and make clear the three kinds of problems that form-analytical translation allows us to solve: the problem of an inform text-tradition, solved by recognition of the forms; the problem of introducing a document, solved by recognition of the distinctive traits of rhetoric and logic that documents exhibit; and the problem of making accessible in a manner visible to the naked eye the rhetorical and logical characteristics of a document. My translations bear the burden of all

[1]In fact, when current work is complete, I shall have done so in three massive sequences of sustained, systematic study, each in its own discipline, literary, historical, history of religions, that is to say, once in the study of literature, the second, of history and history of ideas, and the third time of religion and the history of religion. But this is not the occasion for an intellectual autobiography, which I do not plan to write.

three tasks, and I believe that these tasks are fully carried out by them. In Chapters Two through Seven I discuss with extensive concrete examples the actual practice of translation. There I also spell out through illustrations the principles that have guided my work, both on its own in translating documents not earlier translated and also in comparison with the results, in translation, of those who worked on the same documents that I retranslated.

All of the chapters began as introductions to one or another of my translations of the classics of Judaism; I have revised, reorganized, and edited each one. A small measure of repetition nonetheless may creep in. I beg the reader's indulgence.

I have now covered, for purposes of my address to the relationship between religion and society in the context of the Judaism of the Dual Torah, most of the documents (and all of the important ones) of that Judaism in its formative age, the first seven centuries of the Common Era. Let me now provide an up-to-date catalogue of my translations. Those of the legal classics are as follows:

*A History of the Mishnaic Law of Purities.* Leiden, 1974-1977: Brill. I-XXII.

I. *Kelim. Chapters One through Eleven.* 1974.
II. *Kelim. Chapters Twelve through Thirty.* 1974.
III. *Kelim. Literary and Historical Problems.* 1974.
IV. *Ohalot. Commentary.* 1975.
V. *Ohalot. Literary and Historical Problems.* 1975.
VI. *Negaim. Mishnah-Tosefta.* 1975.
VII. *Negaim. Sifra.* 1975.
VIII. *Negaim. Literary and Historical Problems.* 1975.
IX. *Parah. Commentary.* 1976.
X. *Parah. Literary and Historical Problems.* 1976.
XI. *Tohorot. Commentary.* 1976.
XII. *Tohorot. Literary and Historical Problems.* 1976.
XIII *Miqvaot. Commentary.* 1976.
XIV. *Miqvaot. Literary and Historical Problems.* 1976.
XV. *Niddah. Commentary.* 1976.
XVI. *Niddah. Literary and Historical Problems.* 1976.
XVII. *Makhshirin.* 1977.
XVIII. *Zabim.* 1977.
XIX. *Tebul Yom. Yadayim.* 1977.
XX. *Uqsin. Cumulative Index, Parts I-XX.* 1977.

*The Tosefta. Translated from the Hebrew.* New York, 1977-1980: Ktav. II-VI.

II. *The Tosefta. Translated from the Hebrew. Second Division. Moed.*
III. *The Tosefta. Translated from the Hebrew. Third Division. Nashim.*
IV. *The Tosefta. Translated from the Hebrew. Fourth Division. Neziqin.*
V. *The Tosefta. Translated from the Hebrew. Fifth Division. Qodoshim.*
VI. *The Tosefta. Translated from the Hebrew. Sixth Division. Tohorot.*

Edited: *The Tosefta. Translated from the Hebrew. I. The First Division (Zeraim).* New York, 1985: Ktav.

*The Tosefta: Its Structure and its Sources.* Atlanta, 1986: Scholars Press for Brown Judaic Studies. Reprise of pertinent results in *Purities* I-XXI.

*A History of the Mishnaic Law of Holy Things.* Leiden, Brill: 1979. I-VI.

I. *Zebahim. Translation and Explanation.*
II. *Menahot. Translation and Explanation.*
III. *Hullin, Bekhorot. Translation and Explanation.*
IV. *Arakhin, Temurah. Translation and Explanation.*
V. *Keritot, Meilah, Tamid, Middot, Qinnim. Translation and Explanation.*

*Form Analysis and Exegesis: A Fresh Approach to the Interpretation of Mishnah.* Minneapolis, 1980: University of Minnesota Press.

*A History of the Mishnaic Law of Women.* Leiden, Brill: 1979-1980. I-V.

I. *Yebamot. Translation and Explanation.*
II. *Ketubot. Translation and Explanation.*
III. *Nedarim, Nazir. Translation and Explanation.*
IV. *Sotah, Gittin, Qiddushin. Translation and Explanation.*

*A History of the Mishnaic Law of Appointed Times.* Leiden, Brill: 1981-1983. I-V.

I. *Shabbat. Translation and Explanation.*
II. *Erubin, Pesahim. Translation and Explanation.*
III. *Sheqalim, Yoma, Sukkah. Translation and Explanation.*
IV. *Besah, Rosh Hashshanah, Taanit, Megillah, Moed Qatan, Hagigah. Translation and Explanation.*

*A History of the Mishnaic Law of Damages.* Leiden, Brill: 1983-1985. I-V.

I. *Baba Qamma. Translation and Explanation.*
II. *Baba Mesia. Translation and Explanation.*
III. *Baba Batra, Sanhedrin, Makkot. Translation and Explanation.*
IV. *Shebuot, Eduyyot, Abodah Zarah, Abot, Horayyot. Translation and Explanation.*

*The Mishnah. A New Translation.* New Haven and London, 1987: Yale University Press.

*The Talmud of the Land of Israel. A Preliminary Translation and Explanation.* Chicago: The University of Chicago Press: 1982-1989. IX-XII, XIV-XV, XVII-XXXV.

IX. *Hallah.* 1991
X. *Orlah. Bikkurim.* 1991.
XI. *Shabbat.* 1991.
XII. *Erubin.* 1990.
XIV. *Yoma.* 1990.
XIX. *Megillah.* 1987.
XV. *Sheqalim.* 1990.
XVII. *Sukkah.* 1988.
XVIII. *Besah. Taanit.* 1987.
XX. *Hagigah. Moed Qatan.* 1986.
XXI. *Yebamot.* 1986.
XXII. *Ketubot.* 1985.
XXIII. *Nedarim* 1985.
XXIV. *Nazir.* 1985.
XXIX. *Baba Mesia.* 1984.
XXV. *Gittin.* 1985
XXVI. *Qiddushin.* 1984.
XXVII. *Sotah.* 1984.
XXVIII. *Baba Qamma.* 1984.
XXX. *Baba Batra.* 1984.
XXXI. *Sanhedrin. Makkot.* 1984.
XXXII. *Shebuot.* 1983.
XXXIII. *Abodah Zarah.* 1982.
XXXIV. *Horayot. Niddah.* 1982.

Edited: *In the Margins of the Yerushalmi. Notes on the English Translation.* Chico, 1983: Scholars Press for Brown Judaic Studies.

*Torah from Our Sages: Pirke Avot. A New American Translation and Explanation.* Chappaqua, 1983: Rossel. Paperback edition: 1987.

*The Talmud of Babylonia. An American Translation.* Chico, 1984-1985: Scholars Press for Brown Judaic Studies.
I. *Tractate Berakhot.*
VI. *Tractate Sukkah.*
XVII. *Tractate Sotah.*
XXIII.A. *Tractate Sanhedrin. Chapters I-III.*
XXIII.B. *Tractate Sanhedrin Chapters IV-VIII.*
XXIII.C. *Tractate Sanhedrin Chapters IX-XI.*
XXXII. *Tractate Arakhin.*

Introductions to these works as documents in Judaism include the following:

*A History of the Mishnaic Law of Purities.* Leiden, 1977: Brill. XXI. *The Redaction and Formulation of the Order of Purities in the Mishnah and Tosefta.*

*A History of the Mishnaic Law of Purities.* Leiden, 1977: Brill. XXII. *The Mishnaic System of Uncleanness. Its Context and History.*

*The Mishnah before 70.* Atlanta, 1987: Scholars Press for Brown Judaic Studies. [Reprise of pertinent results of *A History of the Mishnah Law of Purities* Vols. III, V, VIII, X, XII, XIV, XVI, XVII, and XVIII.

*A History of the Mishnaic Law of Holy Things.* Leiden, 1979: Brill. VI. *The Mishnaic System of Sacrifice and Sanctuary.*

*A History of the Mishnaic Law of Women.* Leiden, 1980: Brill. V. *The Mishnaic System of Women.*

*A History of the Mishnaic Law of Appointed Times.* Leiden, 1981: Brill. V. *The Mishnaic System of Appointed Times.*

*A History of the Mishnaic Law of Damages.* Leiden, 1985: Brill. V. *The Mishnaic System of Damages*

*The Talmud of the Land of Israel. A Preliminary Translation and Explanation.* Chicago: The University of Chicago Press: 1983. XXXV. *Introduction. Taxonomy.*

*Invitation to the Talmud. A Teaching Book.* New York, 1973: Harper & Row. Second printing, 1974. Paperback edition, 1975. Reprinted: 1982. Second edition, completely revised, San Francisco, 1984: Harper & Row. Paperback edition: 1988. Japanese translation: Tokyo, 1989: Yamamoto Shoten.

*Judaism. The Evidence of the Mishnah.* Chicago, 1981: University of Chicago Press. *Choice,* "Outstanding Academic Book List 1982-1983." Paperback edition, 1984. Second printing, 1985. Third printing, 1986. Second edition, augmented: Atlanta, 1987: Scholars Press for Brown Judaic Studies. *Hayyahadut le'edut hammishnah.* Hebrew translation of *Judaism. The Evidence of the Mishnah.* Tel Aviv, 1987: Sifriat Poalim. Italian translation: Torino, 1990: Editrice Marietti.

*Judaism without Christianity. An Introduction to the System of the Mishnah.* Hoboken, 1989: Ktav Publishing House. Abbreviated version of *Judaism: The Evidence of the Mishnah.*

*Judaism in Society: The Evidence of the Yerushalmi. Toward the Natural History of a Religion.* Chicago, 1983: The University of Chicago Press. *Choice,* "Outstanding Academic Book List, 1984-1985."

*Judaism and Scripture: The Evidence of Leviticus Rabbah.* Chicago, 1986: The University of Chicago Press. Fresh translation of Margulies' text and systematic analysis of problems of composition and redaction.] Jewish Book Club Selection, 1986.

*Judaism: The Classical Statement. The Evidence of the Bavli.* Chicago, 1986: University of Chicago Press. *Choice,* "Outstanding Academic Book List, 1987."

*Judaism and Story: The Evidence of The Fathers According to Rabbi Nathan.* Chicago, 1990: University of Chicago Press.

*Writing with Scripture: The Authority and Uses of the Hebrew Bible in the Torah of Formative Judaism.* Philadelphia, 1989: Fortress Press.

*The Making of the Mind of Judaism.* Atlanta, 1987: Scholars Press for Brown Judaic Studies.

*The Formation of the Jewish Intellect. Making Connections and Drawing Conclusions in the Traditional System of Judaism.* Atlanta, 1988: Scholars Press for Brown Judaic Studies.

*The Mishnah. An Introduction.* Northvale, N.J., 1989: Jason Aronson, Inc.

*The Philosophical Mishnah.* Volume I. *The Initial Probe.* Atlanta, 1989: Scholars Press for Brown Judaic Studies.

*The Philosophical Mishnah.* Volume II. *The Tractates' Agenda. From Abodah Zarah to Moed Qatan.* Atlanta, 1989: Scholars Press for Brown Judaic Studies.

*The Philosophical Mishnah.* Volume III. *The Tractates' Agenda. From Nazir to Zebahim.* Atlanta, 1989: Scholars Press for Brown Judaic Studies.

*The Philosophical Mishnah.* Volume IV. *The Repertoire.* Atlanta, 1989: Scholars Press for Brown Judaic Studies.

*The Philosophy of Judaism. The First Principles.* Under consideration by Johns Hopkins University Press.

My translations of midrash-compilations are as follows:

Leviticus Rabbah: *Judaism and Scripture: The Evidence of Leviticus Rabbah.* Chicago, 1986: The University of Chicago Press.

*Genesis Rabbah. The Judaic Commentary on Genesis. A New American Translation.* Atlanta, 1985: Scholars Press for Brown Judaic Studies. I. *Genesis Rabbah. The Judaic Commentary on Genesis. A New American Translation. Parashiyyot One through Thirty-Three. Genesis 1:1-8:14.*

*Genesis Rabbah. The Judaic Commentary on Genesis. A New American Translation.* Atlanta, 1985: Scholars Press for Brown Judaic Studies. II. *Genesis Rabbah. The Judaic Commentary on Genesis. A New American Translation. Parashiyyot Thirty-Four through Sixty-Seven. Genesis 8:15-28:9.*

*Genesis Rabbah. The Judaic Commentary on Genesis. A New American Translation.* Atlanta, 1985: Scholars Press for Brown Judaic Studies. III. *Genesis Rabbah. The Judaic Commentary on Genesis. A New American Translation. Parashiyyot Sixty-Eight through One Hundred. Genesis 28:10-50:26.*

*Sifra. The Judaic Commentary on Leviticus. A New Translation. The Leper. Leviticus 13:1-14:57.* Chico, 1985: Scholars Press for Brown Judaic Studies. With a section by Roger Brooks. Based on *A History of the Mishnaic Law of Purities. VI. Negaim. Sifra.*

*Sifré to Numbers. An American Translation.* I. *1-58.* Atlanta, 1986: Scholars Press for Brown Judaic Studies.

*Sifré to Numbers. An American Translation.* II. *59-115.* Atlanta, 1986: Scholars Press for Brown Judaic Studies. III. *116-161:* William Scott Green.

*The Fathers According to Rabbi Nathan. An Analytical Translation and Explanation.* Atlanta, 1986: Scholars Press for Brown Judaic Studies.

*Pesiqta deRab Kahana. An Analytical Translation and Explanation.* I. *1-14.* Atlanta, 1987: Scholars Press for Brown Judaic Studies.

*Pesiqta deRab Kahana. An Analytical Translation and Explanation.* II. *15-28. With an Introduction to Pesiqta deRab Kahana.* Atlanta, 1987: Scholars Press for Brown Judaic Studies.

For Pesiqta Rabbati, *From Tradition to Imitation. The Plan and Program of Pesiqta deRab Kahana and Pesiqta Rabbati.* Atlanta, 1987: Scholars Press for Brown Judaic Studies.

*Sifré to Deuteronomy. An Analytical Translation.* Atlanta, 1987: Scholars Press for Brown Judaic Studies. I. *Pisqaot One through One Hundred Forty-Three. Debarim, Waethanan, Eqeb, Re'eh.*

*Sifré to Deuteronomy. An Analytical Translation.* Atlanta, 1987: Scholars Press for Brown Judaic Studies. II. *Pisqaot One Hundred Forty-Four through Three Hundred Fifty-Seven. Shofetim, Ki Tese, Ki Tabo, Nesabim, Ha'azinu, Zot Habberakhah.*

*Sifré to Deuteronomy. An Introduction to the Rhetorical, Logical, and Topical Program.* Atlanta, 1987: Scholars Press for Brown Judaic Studies.

*Sifra. An Analytical Translation.* Atlanta, 1988: Scholars Press for Brown Judaic Studies. I. *Introduction* and *Vayyiqra Dibura Denedabah* and *Vayiqqra Dibura Dehobah.*

*Sifra. An Analytical Translation.* Atlanta, 1988: Scholars Press for Brown Judaic Studies. II. *Sav, Shemini, Tazria, Negaim, Mesora,* and *Zabim*

*Sifra. An Analytical Translation.* Atlanta, 1988: Scholars Press for Brown Judaic Studies. III. *Aharé Mot, Qedoshim, Emor, Behar,* and *Behuqotai.*

*Uniting the Dual Torah: Sifra and the Problem of the Mishnah.* Cambridge and New York, 1989: Cambridge University Press.

*Sifra in Perspective: The Documentary Comparison of the Midrashim of Ancient Judaism* Atlanta, 1988: Scholars Press for Brown Judaic Studies.

*Mekhilta Attributed to R. Ishmael. An Analytical Translation.* Atlanta, 1988: Scholars Press for Brown Judaic Studies. I. *Pisha, Beshallah, Shirata, and Vayassa.*

*Mekhilta Attributed to R. Ishmael. An Analytical Translation.* Atlanta, 1988: Scholars Press for Brown Judaic Studies. II. *Amalek, Bahodesh, Neziqin, Kaspa and Shabbata.*

*Mekhilta Attributed to R. Ishmael. An Introduction to Judaism's First Scriptural Encyclopaedia.* Atlanta, 1988: Scholars Press for Brown Judaic Studies.

*Lamentations Rabbah. An Analytical Translation.* Atlanta, 1989: Scholars Press for Brown Judaic Studies.

*Esther Rabbah. An Analytical Translation.* Atlanta, 1989: Scholars Press for Brown Judaic Studies.

My analytical studies of, and introductions to, these midrash-compilations have set forth some of the results of the comparison of one midrash-compilation to another, that is, comparative Midrash in redactional context. I have further shown that a variety of Midrash-compilations constitute well-crafted and cogent documents, each with its distinctive medium, method, and message. These studies include the following:

*The Integrity of Leviticus Rabbah. The Problem of the Autonomy of a Rabbinic Document.* Chico, 1985: Scholars Press for Brown Judaic Studies.

*Comparative Midrash: The Plan and Program of Genesis Rabbah and Leviticus Rabbah.* Atlanta, 1986: Scholars Press for Brown Judaic Studies.

*From Tradition to Imitation. The Plan and Program of Pesiqta deRab Kahana and Pesiqta Rabbati.* Atlanta, 1987: Scholars Press for Brown Judaic Studies. With a fresh translation of Pesiqta Rabbati *Pisqaot* 1-5, 15.

*Canon and Connection: Intertextuality in Judaism.* Lanham, 1986: University Press of America. *Studies in Judaism* Series.

*Midrash as Literature: The Primacy of Documentary Discourse.* Lanham, 1987: University Press of America. *Studies in Judaism* series.

*Invitation to Midrash: The Working of Rabbinic Bible Interpretation. A Teaching Book.* San Francisco, 1988: Harper & Row.

*What Is Midrash?* Philadelphia, 1987: Fortress Press.

*Judaism and Story: The Evidence of The Fathers According to Rabbi Nathan.* Chicago, 1990: University of Chicago Press.

*The Foundations of Judaism. Method, Teleology, Doctrine.* Philadelphia, 1983-1985: Fortress Press. I-III. I. *Midrash in Context. Exegesis in Formative Judaism.* Second printing: Atlanta, 1988: Scholars Press for Brown Judaic Studies.

*The Oral Torah. The Sacred Books of Judaism. An Introduction.* San Francisco, 1985: Harper & Row. Paperback, 1987. Bnai Brith Jewish Book Club Selection, 1986.

Edited: *Scriptures of the Oral Torah. Sanctification and Salvation in the Sacred Books of Judaism.* San Francisco, 1987: Harper & Row. Jewish Book Club Selection, 1988.

*Judaism and Christianity in the Age of Constantine. Issues of the Initial Confrontation.* Chicago, 1987: University of Chicago Press.

*Writing with Scripture: The Authority and Uses of the Hebrew Bible in the Torah of Formative Judaism.* Philadelphia, 1989: Fortress Press.

*Why No Gospels in Talmudic Judaism?* Atlanta, 1988: Scholars Press for Brown Judaic Studies.

*Genesis and Judaism: The Perspective of Genesis Rabbah. An Analytical Anthology.* Atlanta, 1986: Scholars Press for Brown Judaic Studies.

*Christian Faith and the Bible of Judaism.* Grand Rapids, 1987: Wm. B. Eerdmans Publishing.

*Comparative Midrash II. The Plan and Program. Lamentations Rabbah and Esther Rabbah I.* Atlanta, 1989: Scholars Press for Brown Judaic Studies.

The remaining midrash-compilations of late antiquity, as identified by Moses D. Herr, "Midrash," *Encyclopaedia Judaica* 11:1511ff., are Ruth Rabbah and Song Rabbah. Since the prevailing consensus assigns these works to the period of late antiquity, that is, prior to the rise of Islam, I shall in due course attend to them.

Among my colleagues at Brown University, my work of translation has benefited especially from conversations with Professor Ernest S. Frerichs. This book was his idea. He further has made one of his principal scholarly interests the study of Bible translations into

English and other languages. Alert to the diverse possibilities and intentionalities of translation of the Hebrew Scriptures, he has helped me gain perspective on my work and its problems.

My other colleagues close at hand, Professors Wendell S. Dietrich, Calvin Goldscheider, David Hirsch, and Alan Zuckerman took a keen interest in this work and encouraged me when it seemed daunting. On all matters having to do with translation and representation, I talk from day to day with Professor William Scott Green, University of Rochester. I keep in touch, moreover, from week to week, with Professors Marvin Fox, Brandeis University, Alan J. Avery-Peck, Tulane University, Paul V. McCracken Flesher, Northwestern University, and Roger Brooks, University of Notre Dame. Engaged in a counterpart project of cultural mediation, Professor Andrew M. Greeley through his scholarly books and articles and also through his novels has taught me much about the problems of translating from one world of thought and language to another.

JACOB NEUSNER

September 1, 1989

*The Institute for Advanced Study*
*Princeton, New Jersey 08540 USA*

# Introduction

I call all my translations "analytical," so let me explain briefly what I mean by "an analytical translation." It is one in which I make immediately visible to the naked eye the principal and indicative literary traits of the Hebrew, so highlighting the distinctive character of rhetoric and logic of the original. I paragraph the whole units of thought, from the smallest building blocks of discourse upward, and indicate the larger compositions, their beginnings and endings. On the basis of that presentation, readers may perform their own form-analyses, inquiries into modes of logical discourse, and other studies that tell us, in aesthetics as much as in theology, the authorship's message and meaning. For any distinction between method and message, form and meaning, obliterates the power of discourse attained in this compilation – as in any other component of the canon of Judaism.

The foundation of my analytical translation is the reference system (to which I make reference again in some of the papers). My reference system allows identification of each complete unit of thought or other irreducible minimum of discourse, e.g., a verse of Scripture. On that basis we may clearly perceive the formal traits of each composite or composition (as the case may be). Let me take as my example Lamentations Rabbah. Until now, to refer to our document we had to use a rather complex system, which distinguished *petihtaot* from *parashiyyot,* and, within *parashayyot,* relied on chapter and verse and then a number, thus I.I.16 stood for the sixteenth among all of the comments in Lamentations Rabbah on Lam. 1:1. This seemed to me not felicitous, since a translation of a given text should number in one and the same way all of that document's components. Otherwise ready-reference is not feasible (unless, of course, one already knows the text that is translated). Hence I have divided the whole of any document I have translated into chapters, whether (in the case of Lamentations Rabbah) a short *petihta* or a very long *parashah.* I further divided the *parashiyyot* into chapters by reference to the verse that is treated, e.g., Lamentations Rabbah to Lam. 1:1 forms a single chapter, then

Lamentations Rabbah to Lam. 1:2 likewise. I formed the whole into a single undifferentiated system.

The real issue of an analytical translation is internal to these chapters. Once I have my Roman numeral, that is, for a given complete unit of material, how do I divide it up? I signify with a small (lower-case) Roman numeral the principal components of a given chapter, of which there may be only one or two. That is indicated by an Arabic numeral, thus **XXXV:i.1** alludes to the first major division of the thirty-fifth chapter of the book (which happens to be Lamentations Rabbah to Lam. 1:1). The Arabic numeral then identifies what I conceive to be a complete argument, proposition, syllogism, or fully worked out exegetical exercise (a whole thought). Finally, I point to what I maintain is the smallest whole unit of thought – e.g., a sentence or a major component of a sentence, a verse of Scripture, a constituent clause of a complex thought, and the like. This is indicated by a letter. Hence **I:I.1.A** alludes to the opening whole unit of thought, in the case at hand, the citation of the base-verse, deriving from what happens to be Petihta One.

By indicating in a thorough way the divisions of discourse, from the smallest whole unit of thought upward, I make possible referring to each component of the document, short of individual words or incomplete clauses, and therefore analyzing the building of each complete thought, proposition, and the like. Everything else rests upon this system. Its utility for form-analysis has been amply demonstrated in all my works, listed presently. In the planned introduction to this compilation, all analysis rests on the complete, detailed account of what I conceive to be all the building-blocks of discourse and thought, smallest to largest.

My purpose throughout therefore has been to make possible analytical studies. By isolating the smallest whole units of thought and then showing how they comprise propositional discourse, and also by highlighting through fixed formulas in English the formal traits of the original, my translation allows for critical inquiry that a translation lacking a reference system does not. Unlike all prior translators of all rabbinic documents of late antiquity into all languages, I offer the text not as a sequence of undifferentiated columns of words. Rather, I represent the Hebrew as a set of distinct and discrete compositions, put together in one way, rather than in some other, and bearing formal and rhetorical traits of a particular sort, rather than some other. That has been my contribution, and while I am confident that corrections and improvements will render my translations still more accurate than they already are, the step forward represented by them will mark a new era in the translating of rabbinic classics.

Furthermore, in my commentary for my translations, I take up, item by item, the indicative traits of each entry and, further, the principles of composition and redaction of one entry with the others fore and aft. In this way I set the stage for analytical studies of the document, such as cannot be carried on and have not been carried on, on the basis of the earlier translation. The reason I believe a fresh translation is required is that, on the basis of prior work of translation, some of it genuinely admirable, no analytical studies of this document are possible. I expand on this point in the nine papers in this book. Most of them have been scattered in various volumes of my translations; some of my theory of translation has never been articulated at all.. As the work concludes, I have decided to spell out in one place what I have been trying to accomplish.

My predecessors in representing the rabbinic classics in other languages (including Modern Hebrew) have proved reticent about explaining their purpose and program. Many of them did not even bother to introduce the documents they were translating, as though the translation itself bore the burden of definition and explanation. And those who have introduced their documents have tended to paraphrase the contents, as we see in my specimen-case, Reuven Hammer's *Introduction* to his translation of Sifré to Deuteronomy, reproduced in part in the Appendix. But he is not the worst instance; he is rather exemplary of problems characteristic among all prior translators into all languages, and the problems that are exemplified cover not only their translations but also their introductions to their documents.

The more I reflect upon the character of all prior translations as well as translations in our own day by others, outside of my circle, indeed, the more I wonder what earlier and other scholars could have had in mind – and today can have in mind – in presenting the text as they did: without a trace of a reference system, without the slightest attention to the indicative marks of style and form and even beginnings and endings of sentences, paragraphs, and completed arguments ("chapters"). And I conclude, they had nothing more in mind than to present the contents of the text. But there is much more to be known about any rabbinic writing, and through correct, which is to say analytical, translation, the indicative traits of style and form can make clear, even to the naked eye, much of the inner structure and program of the rabbinic writings.

Questions of inquiry into the traits of the constituents of the compilation and the plan and program of composition, the types of form and patterning of language and syntax, the logics of cogent discourse, even the topical and propositional program – none of these indicative traits can be analyzed in a text that consists of long columns of undifferentiated type, broken up into unmarked paragraphs. The problem is not only that my predecessors without exception supplied no reference system whatsoever. They also presented an utterly undifferentiated text, so that it is difficult to conduct such studies as require differentiation between and among sizable constituents of the whole. Nor on the basis of their translations can we tell where they think one unit of thought ends and another begins or why one unit of completed thought has been set next to another, rather than somewhere else. In order to make possible a variety of descriptive and analytical studies of a variety of documents, therefore, I found it necessary to translate many of them once again. I do not claim to have improved in any important way on the exegetical and philological work of most of my predecessors (though some reviewers have suggested that I indeed have done so, and others have not agreed).[1] Overall, wherever I had access to prior work on documents, I have found it admirable, but only on the re-presentation of the document in a more suitable way.

While taking full advantage of earlier readings of the documents, therefore, I have found it necessary to retranslate entire compositions. My intent has been to offer a clear account of the basic statement of the

---

[1]In various components of my *Garland Library of Formative Judaism* (New York, 1990: Garland Publishing), in twenty-one volumes, I have reproduced all of the sustainedly hostile reviews of books of mine. Read all together, they offer welcome guidance to areas that can stand improvement. It would make matters somewhat clearer if reviewers would differentiate between obvious error, which is to be corrected, and differences of opinion, which may be negotiated or allowed to stand; but that is asking what is rarely given. The mode of discourse deemed plausible in these writings need not detain us; readers will readily realize that that mode is conventional and not specific to the books under discussion or particularly provoked by them. Indeed, that convention of uncivil discourse has deplorably denied these hostile reviews much of a hearing outside of very narrow circles of like-minded persons, most of them in a few isolated places. But, since in all cases I was able to absorb and make use of the important criticism (for instance, in my *In the Margins of the Yerushalmi. Glosses on the English Translation* (Chico, 1983: Scholars Press for Brown Judaic Studies), what was productive in the writings about my books, including my translations, of Zeitlin, Lieberman, and some rather junior scholars in Jerusalem and in the yeshiva-world, has assuredly been taken into account and used. These reviews should not be dismissed as crackpot merely because they are cranky. There is much of value in them, as I explain in *In the Margins.* That is why, when given the chance to reprint them all together in one place, I did so.

authorship of each piece of writing, together with an identification of the components of their writing classified from the smallest whole units of discourse on upward to completed and coherent statements. That program accounts for my analytical system, which marks each smallest whole unit of thought with a letter, completed propositions of thought (which we might call "paragraphs") with an Arabic numeral, and entire cogent statements or arguments with a Roman numeral. In addition to contributing the first usable analytical marking system for every sentence, I also supply a numbering system in sequence, beginning to the end of the document, for every completed unit of thought (*petihta* and *parashah* as well), simply by enumerating every chapter in sequence, beginning to end. Now people do not have to find a passage identified only as (in the case of Lamentations Rabbah) "see Petihta 24" – which runs on for nine pages!

A mark of the primitive stage at which we stand in the study of the entirety of the rabbinic corpus out of late antiquity is the necessity, at the end of two hundred years of the so-called *Wissenschaft des Judenthums*, to provide a useful system of identifying each sentence of each paragraph of each chapter of each document, something that, for Scripture, we have had for many centuries. The system of identifying the sentences, paragraphs, and chapters that I have devised now applies to nearly the whole of rabbinic literature of late antiquity, that is, from the Mishnah through the Bavli, with successive tractates of the Bavli coming out in our *The Talmud of Babylonia. An American Translation* (Scholars Press for Brown Judaic Studies), alongside the nearly complete *Talmud of the Land of Israel. A Preliminary Translation and Explanation* (University of Chicago Press). I anticipate that, however the exegesis of the text may improve upon my basic translation and philological progress revise and correct details of sense imputed to words and phrases, the fundamental analytical structure I have identified and presented will endure, as it has for every other document in the rabbinic canon translated by me.

So far as I know, no other reference system has been offered to compete with mine. To be sure, even now, rabbinic texts are presented, in Hebrew, German, and English, lacking any reference system beyond "chapter" and translation-page-number. But that only confirms my claim to have invented the only useful and simple reference system. I am not surprised that others may find their own reference systems; that is to be encouraged. I am astonished that, this late in the history of modern scholarship on Judaism, texts still appear from otherwise reputable publishers without even a pretense at a reference system, a work to which I devote considerable attention, because I find it exemplary of what is at fault in all other translations; Hammer's *Sifré to Deuteronomy*, published by Yale University Press, is a case in point. But similar, retrograde attitudes prevail among supposedly *scientific* translators into the Western languages: German, French, English, and now, even Spanish.

The plan of this book is simple. First I present my overall theory of the types of translation of a rabbinic classic that present themselves to me. Then in Chapter Two I compare my translation of a few pages of the Talmud of Babylonia with that of Leo Jung, showing the differences; these then illustrate two different approaches to translation. In Chapter Three I set forth yet another type of translation as explained in my theoretical statement. Part Two, encompassing Chapters Four through Seven, compares my translations with those by others who have worked on the same writings. These are as follows: Braude and Kapstein on Pesiqta deRab Kahana, who follow a theory of translation as paraphrase; Judah Goldin's translation of The Fathers According to Rabbi Nathan, who has no clear notion of his audience at all and translates elegantly but purposelessly; Paul Levertoff, who provides a précis rather than a translation (M. Schwab's French translation of the Yerushalmi likewise skips pages without saying so); and, to exemplify the many reference-translations (into which Goldin's falls, as a matter of fact), I discuss Reuven Hammer's Sifré to Deuteronomy. It seems to me only fair to evaluate two or more approaches to the same problem, rather than judging each in isolation from all others.

Finally, in Part Three, Chapters Eight, Nine, and Ten, I specify the scholarly issues that a translation can and should address. I try to explain precisely why an analytical translation makes possible work of considerable importance and show, as best I can, how this is done. In explaining what I conceive to be at stake in the work of translation, I hope to set forth compelling reasons for doing the work in the manner I do it,[2] rather than in the way it has been done to date by others. In

---

[2]My students' translations of Mishnah- and Tosefta-tractates, of course, have followed the methods I taught them. The Bavli tractates translated by Alan J. Avery-Peck, *Besah*, Martin S. Jaffee, *Horayot*, and Peter J. Haas, *Meilah and Tamid*, (all: Atlanta: Scholars Press for Brown Judaic Studies), and the Yerushalmi tractates by Avery-Peck, *Terumot* and also *Shebiit*, Jaffee, *Maaserot*, Roger Brooks, *Peah* and also *Maaser Sheni*, Tzvee Zahavy, *Berakhot*, Richard S. Sarason, *Demai*, Irving Mandelbaum, *Kilayim*, (all: Chicago: University of Chicago Press) follow the same pattern as I have established. But outside of our circle I cannot point to other work that addresses the issues raised in this book and solves the problems I have worked out, whether in my way or in some other way. My hope is that the new Spanish school of translators of midrash-compilations will take seriously the problem of a

these pages I mean therefore to spell out for the translation of the rabbinic literature the answers to the fundamental issue facing all humanistic learning: *why this, not that.* The answer to that question comprises what I offer as the correct theory and the sound practice of presenting in American English the classics of Judaism.

---

reference system and do something they find useful to solve it. The German translations have done nothing; the Yerushalmi translation into German (under my nominal editorship for a time, though I was not consulted about a single matter) is as expected erudite but witless.

# Part One

# THE THEORY OF TRANSLATING CLASSICS OF JUDAISM: THE TRANSLATION AS AN INSTRUMENT OF ANALYSIS

# 1

# Toward a General Theory of Translation of the Rabbinic Canon

The classic and enduring texts of humanity undergo translation in each succeeding age. For to make acquisition of the heritage of the past, each new generation takes up the task of confronting and making its own what the prior civilization has bequeathed to it. An exception to that general rule of culture until the present day has been the sacred literature of the canon of Judaism. Excluding only the Hebrew Scriptures (Tanakh, "Old Testament"), no text originally in Hebrew or Aramaic of the entire Judaic canon so far as I know reached a foreign language, except for Latin, before the nineteenth century. The reason is that, before modern times, Jews took for granted only they would wish to receive and revere the literary heritage of their people. They further assumed that all male, worthy Jews could learn to read them in the original Hebrew or Aramaic. Learned men translated into, not out of, Hebrew. The act of translation therefore drew a certain opprobrium. Serious scholars would not bother; self-respecting male Jews would master the original language anyhow. The rabbinic heritage belonged to a small group of learned men; translating meant sharing, beyond the limits of the mandarin caste and even of the group, and this was not contemplated.

In the later nineteenth century in Germany and France, and in the twentieth century in Britain and the USA, by contrast, numerous scholars have turned to the task of transmitting the heritage of Judaism to an audience of Western Jews of both genders and also – and clearly by intention – to non-Jews. Major translations found audiences and markets, so, as a matter of fact, a considerable reception among non-Jews and Jews awaited the results of translation. The Mishnah reached most of the Western languages, the Babylonian Talmud came into

German and three times into English (Rodkinson, Soncino, Brown Judaic Studies now in progress), and the Palestinian Talmud into French at the end of the nineteenth century, in German (partially) in the past decade or so, and English just now in my and my students' complete translation. Most (though by no means all) of the compilations and compositions of scriptural exegesis produced by the rabbis of late antiquity and medieval times ("midrashim")[1] exist in German and English. Some have been translated into English two or even three times. Midrash-translations of a high quality as to philological erudition into Spanish and Italian are now appearing. By the end of this century, all of those classics of the canon of Judaism that were completed by the end of late antiquity will have come into the English (mainly, the American) language. My own part is signified in the preface of this book. For the canonical writings from the Mishnah through the Bavli I have done most of the work of translating what was not in English and retranslating what was.

Why have we done what no former generation found urgent, and why has the work proved encompassing in ambition and scope? It is not because fewer people read Hebrew than read Hebrew in Poland or in Russia, though that is surely the fact. The reason our generation found itself called to this work is that there is a sizable audience, both Jewish and gentile, and there also is a significant corps of competent and interested translators available to do the work. People want to read these documents, whose counterparts in the past did not (or who had no counterparts in prior cultures of Judaism and of world religions). And there are people who want to present these documents in their native languages, American English for example, in the assumption that the classics of Judaism have an important contribution to make to the formation of culture and society in our own time.

---

[1]I do not deal with the translation of the Targumim, which do not seem to me definitively to be classified as documents of the Judaism of the Dual Torah in particular. It suffices to say that the Targumim are now coming into English at a very rapid pace, with the translations based on very reliable Hebrew versions, and Neofiti is in all the Western languages. The progress of Targumic studies in philology and text-criticism has made possible the beginnings of serious work on these documents from the perspective of history and the history of religion, but, apart from some very basic exercises, the studies completed to date are episodic and not at all systematic. I should point to the Judaism(s) represented by the various, discrete Targum-writings as one of the great frontiers in the study of the history of Judaism within the history of religion. Fortunately, my former student, Paul V. McC. Flesher, has undertaken sustained work in this area, and I should anticipate that in a decade or so, these remarks will prove obsolete.

This renewed interest in cultural mediation such as translation characterizes both religious and secular scholarship on Judaism in the State of Israel as well. In passing we take note that many of the documents at hand attract the interest of translators into modern, Israeli Hebrew as well. Translations of both Talmuds into Hebrew and of the more important midrash-compilations – all of Midrash Rabbah, for instance – attest to the importance accorded to providing access to the Judaic classics for the Israeli audience as well. So the issue is not, and therefore never was, merely knowledge of Hebrew as such.

Clearly, therefore, we find a sustained and broad interest in reading the classics of Judaism and in presenting those classics for reading. At stake is a cultural concern, and what we witness is a shift in cultural commitments and policy. To put matters differently, the substantial interest in the labor of moving the old texts from one language and system of thought into another would surprise no one, except, as I said, those many generations of male Jews[2] who took for granted translation was neither necessary nor valuable, in the untested theory that whoever cared knew Hebrew or should learn it. The contrast between the modern interest in restudy through translation and the prior interest in studying without translation requires analysis in its own terms; for my purpose it suffices to note that for translation to matter, much has had to change, and much has changed, in the character of the Jews' culture and of that of the world in which they lived as well.[3]

---

[2]Even today in many *yeshivot,* women are not permitted to study the Talmud of Babylonia and related writings.

[3]When I was a student from 1954 to 1960 at the Jewish Theological Seminary (including a year at the Hebrew University of Jerusalem in 1957-1958), and beginning my earliest experiments at translating the classic texts, I was repeatedly told not to bother. "If people know Hebrew (and Aramaic), they do not need your translation, and if they do not, they will not understand these writings anyhow." Indeed, there was so much pressure against doing so that I set aside any sustained and systematic work for the next twelve years, only renewing it in a systematic way when I reached the conclusion that the Mishnah and the Tosefta had to be completely reread as historical documents. That conclusion, in 1972 (hinted at in my *Eliezer ben Hyrcanus: The Tradition and the Man*) led to the sustained work, beginning in 1972 and reaching its conclusion, I expect, in the early 1990s. Some of the reviews of my Yerushalmi translation even as late as the mid-1980s – all of them by persons who themselves have never undertaken to translate a single document of Judaism! – persistently objected to the very fact of the translation, not only to specific points of disagreement or even error they found in it. Some have wondered whether there was not a prejudice against allowing the world at large access to

Still, a certain snobbery survives in narrow academic circles, Jerusalem, for one, the Jewish rabbinical seminaries, for another. There the labor of translation is not attempted and also not appreciated: why both? "Those who know Hebrew do not need it, and those who do not will never understand anyhow" – so it is argued. But outside of the canon of writings at hand no one debates the question of whether a given text requires more than a single translation into a given language. Great scholars who also are great poets undertake the successive retranslation of every great classic of world literature, whether philosophical or dramatic or poetic. Who can count the number of translations into English alone of the Hebrew Scriptures? It is common that through the work of serious translation great literary creations have come into being, in the case, for instance, of Homer, Plato, and Euripides. None therefore need wonder why someone would translate afresh a classic text of Judaism that already exists in the English language. What requires attention is only the issue of what the latter-day translator wishes to accomplish, that has been left undone by a predecessor.

Now that the sustained labor of translating and retranslating classics defines an important scholarly task in the study of Judaism, we have to examine the various ways in which translation is to be done, which is to say, the purposes of the work, the goals that can be achieved if we do things in one way, rather than in some other. In these pages I want to spell out and also exemplify a variety of theories of translation of rabbinic literature. In the present context, I see no fewer than four available theories of translation, each one of which enjoys its distinctive value. Let me spell them out, so as to place into context the newest effort to translate a classic text of Judaism into the American language. These may be briefly entitled [1] a literary translation, [2] a reference translation, [3] a research translation, made for purposes of analyzing a document, its structure, plan, and purpose, and [4] a conversation translation. I have aimed at producing translations of the second, third, and fourth kind, as the need required.

---

these writings, knowledge of which had formerly been protected for disciples and masters within the rabbinic world alone. In any event there is no scholarly tradition that accords importance and appreciation to the labor of translation, even though, as everyone who has translated knows, a translation happens to form, on its own, a line-by-line commentary to the original. But, I hasten to add, the appreciation for what has been done, marked by the more than satisfactory sales of the various translations and also by the more than gratifying reviews they have received, far outweighs the denigration and rejection expressed by a few.

I do not claim to have produced a literary translation but will point to work that seems to me to transcend the limitations of translation and turn it into art.

[1] A literary translation aims at presenting in English not a literal and exact rendition of the text but an elegant and poetic one. It transmits main ideas, thoughts closely related to, but not in the exact language of, the original. Such a translation aims through the power of the contemporary idiom at winning to the gist of the text a sizable audience of lay readers. Success then means a large and understanding audience. The translator serves as a partner to the original author. My impression is that all efforts at translating poetry fall into this classification. In a later chapter I shall treat the work of William Braude and Judah Goldin in producing literary translations. Goldin seems to have succeeded admirably, in his *Grace after Meals,* (which many regard as his best work), *Song at the Sea* and in his *Fathers According to Rabbi Nathan.* Translations of the liturgy of Judaism, much of it deriving from late antiquity, have yielded more than merely serviceable prose; the work of Jules Harlow under the auspices of the Rabbinical Assembly seems to me noteworthy. For his part, William Braude in some of his earlier work produced good writing. But much of Braude's work, and all of the translating he did with Israel J. Kapstein, is not really translation so much as paraphrase, as we shall observe at some length.

[2] A reference translation, the opposite of the foregoing, provides a succinct and literal account of the original, with few notes of the character of more than brief references. The utility of such a translation is to facilitate quick reference to the original text. It will serve to guide the outsider to a given passage; but not to lead into the heart of matters someone who does not know the original language. Such a purpose, for the aesthetic side, is served by the literary translation. Reference translations discussed in the pages that follow include those for Sifré to Numbers (Levertoff) and Sifré to Deuteronomy (Hammer); I had to retranslate both documents because of the insufficiency of their work, at the same time appreciating the many problems that they solved.[4]

[3] As to research translations, there are two kinds. The first is intended to provide a vast amount of information, the second, to offer

[4]My one-volume translation of the Mishnah and the six of Tosefta are of course reference translations, but they are based upon extended commentaries, forty-three volumes in fact, as listed in the preface. My translations of the Yerushalmi and Bavli are conversation translations, and all of my translations are analytical.

access to the structure and form of a document. I have done both kinds of translations of a research character, for the Mishnah and the Tosefta on the one side, for the midrash-compilations, among other writings, on the other. Indeed, all of my translations are meant to be analytical, as I have explained in the preface of this book.

As analytical translations, all of mine fall into the category of research translations, even though I place a low priority on problems of philology, which seem to me only of modest importance in translating classic texts. Issues of form, logic, structure, order, and program take priority, and few research translations attend to issues other than those of meanings of words and phrases. Indeed, some research editions – text and commentary – prove nearly useless except for reference purposes, because they are overburdened with information and lack a coherent structure and order; Saul Lieberman's vast edition and commentary to four of the six divisions of Tosefta has been justly called a garbage pail because of its disorder and ostentatious erudition, though in the mass of materials are numerous important bits and pieces of information.

For the substantive side of things, the research translation, the exact opposite of the reference translation, serves admirably. Such a translation draws together into one place every piece of information that appears to pertain to the passage at hand. Philological, historical, textual issues intervene into the text. The scholar, particularly one who works in an area other than that of the text at hand, finds in such a translation enormous assistance. The research translation further will address the issue of variant text-traditions of the text at hand, so that diverse manuscripts will come to testify to the original sense and wording of the passage.

[4] Standing apart from the first three types of translation, the conversation translation aims at one thing only, and that is, clear comprehension not only of the words but also of the sense of the classic text. My translations of the Talmud of Babylonia and the Talmud of the Land of Israel are of this kind. In the third paper of this excursus, I give a sizable sample of the latter. Alan J. Avery-Peck's and Martin Jaffee's translations of tractates of both the Yerushalmi and Bavli provide still better examples of conversation translations at their fullest.[5] That these form major contributions to scholarship seems to me self-evident.

---

[5]See Martin Jaffee, *The Talmud of Babylonia: An American Translation. XXVI: Treactate Horayot*, and Alan J. Avery-Peck, *The Talmud of Babylonia. An American Translation. VII: Tractate Besah* (both: Atlanta, 1987, 1988: Scholars Press for Brown Judaic Studies).

What exactly do I mean by a "conversation translation"? It is an effort to "talk the reader through" the text, clearly distinguishing language added by the translator from the original words of the text. In this way the translator renders accessible the distinctive message and mode of thought of the ancient text. Who will want such a translation? The same sort of reader who responds to the literary sort of translation, but with a difference. The reader at hand wants access to not only the gist of discourse but the mode and medium. It is insufficient to such a reader to know what, in general, the text wishes to tell us. Such a reader wishes to know the message in relation to the medium.

Let me now spell out my views of these available theories of translation and explain my preference for the fourth one in particular.

The reference translation I deem inadequate because it is of very limited use since it leaves the text unexplained. The fact that the uninterpreted text, unadorned with amplification, can be used for any scholarly purpose testifies to the superficiality of interest in the rabbinic classics among those who propose to make use of them for their research, e.g., in New Testament studies. Users of compendia of sayings and stories in rabbinic literature relevant to New Testament Gospels, Strack-Billerbeck's compilation, for instance, very commonly copy a story from a reference translation without paying any attention to its context or purpose. The result is a kind of puerile learning of no serious use whatever.

The research translation has merit; since it stands as a convenient source for whatever is relevant (and much that is not relevant) to the particular text subject to translation. But it is not a great deal more useful than the reference translation for those whose principal interest is in what this text says and what it means. Only a reference translation, putting down on paper only the corresponding words in the other language so that people may look things up and pick and choose what may be useful, justifies an essentially unadorned translation, a simple "rendition" from one language to the other. A research translation meant to raise and solve all the problems, philological and linguistic, textual and lexicographical, historical and theological, ranging here, there, and everywhere, with endless notes and a dazzling display of erudition – such a translation seems to me of equally limited use but for a different reason.

For someone opening a research translation will find overwhelming the limitless ranges of erudite discourse and so lose sight of the issue at hand. For a translation of the Talmud of Babylonia, for example, that issue is the protracted and brilliant exercise in practical reason and applied logic which is the Babylonian Talmud at its most interesting, if also its most difficult. An unformed and purposeless collection of information will hardly render accessible that reason and logic; it can only obscure whatever the text means to say. The *El Am Talmud,* published by Conservative Judaism for purposes of study by the pious, exemplifies the obscurantism involved in this sort of celebration of information for its own sake. (The fact that most of the information provided in that deplorable version of the Bavli happens to be wrong need not detain us. When people celebrate facts, which facts they choose for the purpose hardly makes much difference.)

What makes one type of translation better than some other? The answer seems to me self-evident. The criterion for evaluating a translation among the available types derives in the end from the audience at hand. For whom does one translate the document anyhow? It cannot be only for those able to make sense of the document in its original language. For them, a translation is merely another commentary. Lacking all canonical status, in the acutely theological and nervous atmosphere of the schools in which this particular document is studied, a translation enjoys no standing whatsoever. That does not mean it will not be used. The excellent efforts of the translators of the Babylonian Talmud into German, then into English, have hardly been neglected in the German- and English-speaking world in which the sacred writings of Judaism are studied. But it is foolish to contribute to a world with its own conventions and canonical exegesis a translation which that world claims not to need and forthrightly alleges it does not want. To that world a translation is not a commentary. It is an affront.

On the other hand, if the translator proposes to present the text "to whom it may concern," that is, to no one in particular, then the question arises of *how much* requires explanation. Here there can simply be no end to the matter. In the case of a document that assumes so vast a knowledge of the Hebrew Scriptures and the Mishnah as does the Talmud, even if one quotes the whole of a verse alluded to only by a word or two, should the translator then proceed to interpret that verse? Its context? Its meaning and use in the passage of the Talmud before us? Similarly, if the Talmud rests upon a pericope of the Mishnah that is not cited at all, should the translator merely allude to the passage and expect the reader to look it up? Should the translator cite the passage in full? And if so, how extensive an explanation is required?

As to the discourse of the rabbinic canon, the translation, of course, constitutes a substantial judgment upon the meaning of the text. Where we put a period or a comma, or indicate the end of one major discourse and the start of another, how we break up the undifferentiated columns of words into paragraphs, the paragraphs into sentences, and the sentences into their individual, small units of cognition – these decisions are conveyed in the very simple facts of how we present what we claim to be the meaning of the text. And yet, beyond that simple statement, it is clear, a fair amount of explanation is demanded. How much, or how little, must be explained is not self-evident, and probably will never be readily settled. It is invariably an exercise of judgment and taste. That is why, as I said, the translator has to find a balance between the requirements of intelligibility, indeed, to whom it may concern, on the one side, and the limited possibilities of full and ample presentation of a single text in a single book, on the other. Too much will overwhelm the reader, who will lose sight of the text, which is, after all, at the center of the translation. Too little will puzzle the reader, leaving the text translated but still inaccessible. In the discussions that follow I mean to explain what I have done and also to criticize the work of others,[6] so as to set forth the issues as clearly as I can.

---

[6]If, except for Chapter Two's work on Jung's Arakhin as against mine, I do not discuss the work of the Soncino translators of the Talmud of Babylonia and the principal midrash-compilations under the titles, *The Talmud* and *Midrash Rabbah* (not to mention the Zohar), it is because I do not think anyone today regards the British work of two generations ago as a suitable model. But I hasten to express my respect for those great pioneers. I have used their translations, line by line, whenever I worked on a text that they had already put into English, and for sheer erudition and philological wit, I do not think they have any peers in our language. My constant reference to their work is made explicit throughout my Genesis Rabbah, Leviticus Rabbah, Lamentations Rabbah, and in my Bavli tractate translations as well.

# 2

# Comparing Theories of Translation: Two Approaches to the Rendition of the Talmud of Babylonia

In order to show in a graphic way the different choices confronting a translator, I turn to the Talmud of Babylonia or Bavli. I contrast a reference translation with a conversation translation. This I do by showing how two translators of the same pages of the Bavli have represented precisely the same materials. Specifically, I set side by side two approaches, Leo Jung's and mine, to the translation of Babylonian tractate Arakhin 2A-2B in, first, the version appearing in the great Soncino translation of the Babylonian Talmud produced, for the tractate at hand, by Leo Jung, and second, my version. In this way the difference in the theories governing how the work is to be done becomes vivid. Within the scheme I have laid forth, I should categorize Jung's (and the rest of the Soncino translations) as essentially a reference translation. Mine, clearly, is meant to be a conversation translation. In order to provide a full picture of how Jung explains what is not self-evidently clear in the text, further, I have included those of his footnotes which constitute more than mere references to other texts. The notes follow the extracts.

In order to make clear how I think my approach to translation differs, let me spell out a few of its salient traits.

[1] The single significant trait in what follows is the extensive use of square brackets to add to the flow of discourse those sources alluded to but not cited.

[2] The translation is richly augmented by understanding not made explicit and by rhetorical shifts and turns in no way indicated in the original Aramaic.

To state the theory of translation of this document as simply as I can: Here I propose to talk my way through an account of what the document says – not stated in square brackets but translated into fairly fluent American English – and of what the document means. That is, both what we need to know to make sense of it, and also what we are supposed to conclude on the basis of what the document says and the facts added by me, are supplied. Translation here is a kind of extended conversation, an interchange within the document, with the document, and through the document, and, always, an urgent encounter with the reader.

If I had to make a guess, I should imagine we deal with nothing more than brief notes, notations really, out of which a whole and complete discourse is supposed to be reconstructed by those essentially familiar with the (original) discourse. The Babylonian Talmud is a kind of abbreviated script, a set of cue cards drastically cut down to a minimum of words. But these metaphors are meant only to account for the theory of translation followed here, I mean the theory that out of the sherds and remnants of coherent speech we have to reconstruct and fully reconstitute the (original) coherent discourse, as best we can, whole sentences from key words, whole analyses from truncated allusions.

MISHNAH. [2a] All [persons] are fit to evaluate or to be made the subjects of valuation, are fit to vow [another's worth] or have their worth vowed: – priests, Levites and [ordinary] Israelites, women and slaves. Persons of unknown sex and hermaphrodites are fit to vow [another's worth], or to have their worth vowed, and are fit to evaluate, but they are not fit to be made the subjects of valuation, for the subject of valuation may be only a person definitely either male or female. A deaf-mute, an imbecile, or a minor are fit to have their worth vowed or be made the subject of valuation, but they are not fit to make either a vow [of another's worth] or to evaluate, because they have no mind.

[2A]

A. *All pledge the Valuation [of others] and are subject to the pledge of Valuation [by others].*

B. *vow [the worth of another] and are subject to the vow [of payment of their worth by another]:*

C. *priests and Levites and Israelites, women and slaves.*

D. *A person of doubtful sexual traits and a person who exhibits traits of both sexes vow [the worth of another] and are subject to the vow [of payment of their worth by another], pledge the Valuation [of others], but are not subject to the pledge of Valuation by others,*

E. *for evaluated is only one who is certainly a male or certainly a female.*

F. *A deaf-mute, an imbecile, and a minor are subject to the vow [of payment of their worth by another], and are subject to the pledge of Valuation by others, but do not vow the worth, and do not pledge the Valuation, of others,*

G. *for they do not possess understanding.*

GEMARA. What does [ALL PERSONS] ARE FIT TO EVALUATE mean to include? – It is meant to include one close to manhood who must be examined.[1] What does [ALL][2] ARE FIT TO BE MADE THE SUBJECTS OF VALUATION MEAN TO INCLUDE? – It is meant to include a person disfigured, or one afflicted with boils. For one might have assumed that since Scripture says: *A vow... according to thy valuation,*[3] that only such persons as are fit to be made the subjects of a vow [as regards their worth], are fit to be made subjects of a valuation, and that persons who are unfit to be made subjects of a vow [as regards their worth], are also unfit to be made subjects of a valuation, hence Scripture informs us: *of persons.*[4] i.e., no matter who they be.

[1]*Mufla'* from the root meaning, to make clear, to examine, hence 'one to be examined' as to the purpose for which he made the valuation. Above the age of thirteen such knowledge is taken for granted. Below the age of twelve it is assumed to be absent. During the period from twelve to thirteen the boy is to be subject to questioning. If the examination establishes his knowledge of the purpose of the dedication, his dedication is considered valid, and renders payment obligatory. Otherwise no significance is to be attached during that period to his utterance of the formula: *Erek peloni' alay.*

I. A. [When the framer explicitly refers to] *all,* [in framing the Mishnah-paragraph at hand, saying *All pledge....,*] what [classification of persons does he intend] to encompass, [seeing that in what follows C, he lists the available classifications of persons in any event, and, further, at D-G specifies categories of persons that are excluded. Accordingly, to what purpose does he add the encompassing language, *all,* at the outset?]

B. It serves to encompass a male nearing puberty [who has not yet passed puberty. Such a one is subject to examination to determine whether he grasps the meaning of a vow, such as is under discussion. A child younger than the specified age, twelve years to thirteen, is assumed not to have such understanding, and one older is taken for granted to have it.]

C. [When the framer explicitly frames matters as *all*] *are subject to the pledge of Valuation,* what [classification of persons does he intend] to encompass?

D. It is to encompass a person who is disfigured or afflicted with a skin ailment.

E. [Why in any event should one imagine that persons of that classification would be omitted?] I might have supposed that, since it is written, "A vow... according to your Valuation" (Lev. 27:2), [with Scripture

[2]The first word of the Mishnah ALL is assumed to apply to the four cases enumerated. This word does not seem necessary, the Mishnah might have stated e.g., Priests, Levites and Israelites are fit etc. The additional ALL hence is assumed by the questioner to have implied the inclusion of persons whom, without this inclusion, one might have excluded. Hence the series of questions establishing the identity of the persons included in each case. This discussion leads to the consideration of other passages throughout the Mishnah, in which the word 'all' occurs, and to an explanation of who is included in each statement.

[4]A person disfigured, or afflicted with boils, would fetch no price at all on the market place. In the expression *A vow according to thy valuation*, one might have inferred from this juxtaposition, that a certain fundamental agreement prevailed between cases of *vow* (of one's worth) and of *valuation*, and that therefore a person unfit to have his work vowed (because a vow was redeemable by payment of the market value, which did not exist in the case of a disfigured person) would be unfit to be made the subject of a valuation. But this inference is cancelled by another biblical phrase, which indicates that what is required is but *'persons'*, independent of their physical condition: *When a man shall clearly utter a vow of persons* (*ibid.*).

using as equivalent terms "vow" and "Valuation,"] the rule is that whoever is possessed of worth [e.g., whoever would be purchased for a sum of money in the marketplace, hence excluding the disfigured persons under discussion, who are worthless] also would be subject to a vow of Valuation [at fixed price, such as Scripture specified]. On the other hand, [I might have supposed that] whoever is not possessed of worth also would not be subject to a vow of Valuation.

F. Accordingly, [the formulation of the Mishnah-passage at hand] tells us, [to the contrary, that a pledge of Valuation represents an absolute charge and is not relative to the subject's market-value.]

G. [How does Scripture so signify? When the framer of Scripture refers at Lev. 27:2 to] "persons," [the meaning is that a pledge of Valuation applies] to anyone at all.

What does [ALL PERSONS] ARE FIT TO VOW mean to include? – [The phrase ALL] is needed only for [the clause] 'are fit to have their worth vowed'. What is to be included [in the phrase ALL] ARE FIT TO HAVE THEIR WORTH VOWED? Is it to include persons of unknown sex or hermaphrodites – but they are expressly stated [in our Mishnah]!

H. [When the framer of the Mishnah, further, states that *all*] *vow* [the worth of another], what [classification of persons does he thereby intend] to encompass [seeing that at C we go over the same matter, specifying those who may make such a vow]?

I. It is necessary for him [to specify that all take such a vow] on

Again is it to include a deaf-mute, an imbecile and a minor – they too are expressly stated! And if it is to include a person below the age of one month – that too is expressly mentioned! And again if it is to include an idolator – he too is expressly mentioned! – In reality it is meant to include a person below the age of one month; and the Mishnah states it [by implication] and later on expressly mentions it.[3]

[3]By the redundant ALL, which obviously includes some person or persons, which but for this all-inclusive term, would have been excluded. The particular reason this case rather than any other of the four dealt with is included here Rashi finds in the fact that it is the only one concerning which a controversy exists (*infra 5a*), whence the statement here by implication is of importance in teaching that even the Rabbis who hold that one who is less than a month cannot be subject to evaluation, nevertheless agree that he can have his worth vowed.

account of those concerning whom such a vow is taken.

J. [And along these same lines, when the framer specifies that all] are subject to a vow, what [classification of persons does he thereby intend] to encompass?

K. [Here matters are not so self-evident, for] if the intention is to encompass a person of doubtful sexual traits and a person who exhibits the traits of both sexes, both of those classifications are explicitly stated [in the formulation of the Mishnah-passage itself].

L. And if the intention is to encompass a deaf-mute, an imbecile, and a minor, these classifications also are explicitly stated. [So what can have been omitted in the explicit specification of the pertinent classifications, that the framer of the Mishnah-passage found it necessary to make use of such amplificatory language as *all*?]

M. If, furthermore, the intent was to encompass an infant less than a month old, that classification also is explicitly included [below].

N. If, furthermore, the intent was to encompass an idolator, that classification furthermore is explicitly included as well. [Accordingly, what classification of persons can possibly have been omitted in the framing of the Mishnah-passage at hand, that the author found it necessary to add the emphatic inclusionary language?]

O. In point of fact, [the purpose of adding the emphatic language of inclusion] was to encompass an infant less than a month in age.

P. [The framer of the passage] taught [that such a category is included] and then he went and restated the matter [once again, so as] to make explicit the inclusion of that category.

What does 'All persons are obliged to lay on hands' mean to include?[4] – It is meant to include the heir, and this against the view of R. Judah.[5] What does 'All persons can effect a substitute'[6] mean to include? – That, too, means to include the heir, in contrast to the view of R. Judah. For it was taught: An heir must lay on hands, an heir can effect a substitute. R. Judah says: An heir does not lay on hands, and an heir cannot effect a substitute.

[4]The Gemara proceeds now to discuss all other cases in which a redundant 'all' is to convey some inclusion in the principle of other persons. The laying on of the hands on the head of the animal to be sacrificed conveyed the sense of ownership. It was a duty, hence a question arises in the case of several partners, or in the case of proxy.

[5]R. Judah denied this obligation to an heir. Lev. I, 3 reads: *If he be a burnt offering...he shall lay his hand upon the head.* This, R. Judah argues, expressly limits the duty of laying the hand to the man who offered it, not to his heir, who is freed from his obligation.

[6]Lev. XXVII, 10: *He shall not alter it, nor change it, a good for a bad, or a bad for a good; and if he shall at all change beast for beast, then both it and that for which it is changed shall be holy.* The dispute concerns only the case of an heir in respect of an offering dedicated by his father but all agree that an exchange made by anyone besides the original owner of the sacrifice would have no effect at all, the first animal remaining sacred, the second not being affected by the unauthorized attempt at exchange.

II. A. [When, along these same lines, we find the formulation], *All lay hands [on a beast to be slaughtered, that is, including not only the owner of the beast, who set it aside and consecrated it for the present sacrificial purpose, but also some other party]*, whom do we find included [by the inclusionary language, *all*]?

B. [It is used to indicate] the inclusion of the heir [of the owner of the beast who originally consecrated it, so that the heir of the deceased owner, taking his place vis-à-vis the beast, also may lay hands on the beast and so derive benefit from the sacrifice of that beast, even though he did not originally designate it as holy].

C. And that inclusion does not accord with the position of R. Judah [who maintains that, since Scripture specifies at Lev. 1:3 that the person who has designated the beast as a holy sacrifice "shall lay hands on it," excluded are all other parties, who did not designate the beast as holy. Only the owner of the beast may lay hands, and no one else. In so formulating the rule by using the inclusionary language *all*, the framer of the passage has indicated that he rejects the position of Judah].

D. [And when, at M. Tem. 1:1, we find the formulation,] *All effect an act of substitution* [so consecrating the beast that is supposed to take the place of the originally consecrated beast, in line with Lev. 27:10, but leaving that originally consecrated beast in the status of consecration nonetheless], what category do we find included [by the use of such language]?

E. [Once more], the use of such language indicates the inclusion of the heir [of the owner of the beast, who originally consecrated it, just as at B, above].

F. And that inclusion once more does not accord with the position of

R. Judah [for Lev. 27:10 states, "*He* shall not alter it...," thus referring solely to the owner of the beast, and not to an heir or any other third party].

G. [Now the statements just given accord with] that which has been taught [in a tradition external to the Mishnah but deriving from authorities named in the Mishnah], as follows:

H. An heir lays hands [on a beast originally consecrated by the deceased], an heir effects an act of substitution [in regard to a beast originally consecrated by the deceased].

I. R. Judah says, "An heir does not lay on hands, an heir does not effect an act of substitution."

What is the reason of R. Judah's view? – [Scripture says:] *His offering,*[1] i.e., but not his father's offering. And he infers the rule concerning the commencement of the dedication of the animal from the rule governing its end. Just as at the end of the dedication the heir does not lay on hands, thus also at the beginning[2] he cannot effect a substitute. And the Rabbis? – [Scripture says redundantly:] *And if he shall at all change* – that included the heir. And we infer the rule concerning the end of the dedication from the rule governing the commencement of the dedication. Just as at the beginning of the dedication the heir has power to effect a substitute, so at the end is he obliged to lay his hands on the animal's head.[3] But what do the Rabbis do with *'his offering'*? – [They interpret:] 'his offering', but not the offering of an idolator; *'his offering'*, but not the offering of his neighbor; *'his offering'*, i.e., to include all who have a share[4] in the ownership of a sacrifice in the duty to lay on hands. And R. Judah?[5] – He does not hold that all who have a share in the

J. What is the scriptural basis for the position of R. Judah?

K. "His offering..." (Lev. 3:2, 7, 13: "He shall lay his hand upon the head of his offering") – and not the offering that was set aside by his father.

L. From the rule governing the end of the process of consecration [the laying on of hands] [R. Judah further] derives the rule governing the beginning of the process of consecrating a beast [e.g., through an act of substitution, which indicates that a given beast is substituted for, therefore shares the status of, another beast that already has been consecrated. In this way the beast put forward as a substitution is itself deemed to be sanctified. Accordingly, a single principle governs both stages in the sacrificial process, the designation of the beast as holy and therefore to be sacrificed, e.g., through an act of substitution, and the laying on of hands just prior to the act of sacrificial slaughter itself. Just as the latter action may be performed solely by the owner of the beast, who derives benefit only when ownership share the obligation of laying hands thereon; or, indeed, if he should hold so [2b] he would infer [the exclusion of] idolator and neighbor from one passage,[6] so that two more would remain redundant, from one of which he would infer that *'his offering'* means 'but not that of his father', and from the other that all who have a share in the ownership of a sacrifice are obliged to perform the laying on of hands. But what does R. Judah do with *'If he shall at all change'?* – He needs that to include woman,[7] for it was taught: Since all this chapter is couched in masculine gender, what brings us eventually to include woman? The text stated: *'If he shall at all change'*[8] But [whence do] the Sages [infer this]? – From the [redundant] *'And if'*. And R. Judah? – He does not interpret *'And if'*.[9]

[1]Lev. II, 2, 7 and 13 in connection with the laying on of hands in the case of peace-offerings. V. Rash and Tosaf. a.l.

[2]First an animal is separated for the purpose of being offered on the altar. That is the commencement of its sanctification. At the end, just before the slaying of the animal, the owner lays his hand on its head. R. Judah infers from the regulations at the end, viz., the prohibition for anyone but the owner to lay hands on the head, the inefficacy of the change at the beginning, i.e., his intended exchange has no effect on the animal he wanted to substitute.

[3]The Sages infer from the redundant *'shall at all change'* that even another may effect the substitute and argue from the beginning of the sanctification to the end, hence permit an heir to lay hands on the animal.

[4]The phrase *'his offering'* occurs

the owner of the beast carries it out, so is the rule for the former action.]

M. Accordingly, just as, at the end of the process of consecration, the heir does not lay on hands, so at the beginning of the process of consecration, an heir does not carry out an act of substitution.

N. And as to the position of rabbis [vis-à-vis Judah, who maintain that the heir may do so, how do they read Scripture in such wise as to derive their view?]

O. [Scripture states,] "And if changing, he shall change" (Lev. 27:10) [thus intensively using the same verb twice, with one usage understood to refer to the owner himself, the other usage to some closely related person].

P. [The use of the verbal intensive therefore is meant] to encompass the heir, and, as before, we derive the rule governing the conclusion of the sacrificial process [with the laying on of hands] from the rule governing the commencement of the sacrificial process [the designation of the beast as holy, by its substitution for an already consecrated beast].

Q. Accordingly, just as, at the beginning of the process of consecration, the heir does carry out an act of substitution, so at the end of the process of consecration, the heir does lay on hands.

R. Now [given rabbis' reading of the relevant verses], how do these same rabbis deal with Scripture's reference to "*his* offering" [which in Judah's view makes explicit that only the owner of the beast lays hands on his beast]?

S. They require that specification of Scripture to lay down the rule that [an Israelite] lays hands on his sacrifice, but not on the sacrifice of an idolator, on his sacrifice and not on the sacrifice of his fellow;

T. on his sacrifice, further, to

three times in Lev. III, viz., vv. 2, 7 and 13, and while two of these expressions have a limiting sense, one has an inclusive meaning. Just as *'his'* implies ownership, so must anyone who has a claim to ownership lay his hands on the animal's head. Therefore, every member of a group who offer the animal together must perform the laying on of hands on the part of anyone who shares in it – for which an inclusive interpretation is necessary?

[6]The word *'his'* could exclude both the fellow-Jew and the idolator, since the Scriptural *'his sacrifice'* logically excludes both.

[7]That a woman can effect a substitute in her offering.

[8]Lit., 'if change he shall change' the emphasis is inclusive.

[9]He does not ascribe to that word the implications attributed to it by the Sages. About the limits of such interpretation and the basic suggestions implied in disputes thereon v. D. Hoffman, *Leviticus* I, 9f.

encompass all those who own a share in the sacrificial animal, according to each the right to lay hands upon the beast [of which they are partners].

U. And as to R. Judah? He does not take the view that all those who own a share in the sacrificial animal have a right to.

V. Alternatively, [one may propose that] he does maintain the stated position [concerning the partners in a sacrificial animal].

W. [But] he derives the rule governing [2b] the idolator['s beast] and that of one's fellow from a single verse of Scripture [among the three that make explicit that one lays hands on *his* animal], leaving available for the demonstration of a quite separate proposition two [other] of these same [three] references.

X. [It follows, for Judah's position, that] one of these verses serves to indicate, "*His* offering" and not the offering of his father," and another of the available verses then serves to encompass [among those who indeed may lay hands on the sacrificial beast] all shareholders, according to each of them the right to lay hands on the beast held in common partnership.

Y. [Further exploring the thesis of Judah about the scriptural basis for his view, exactly] how does R. Judah interpret the intensive verb used at Lev. 27:10, "And if changing, he shall change"?

Z. He requires that usage to encompass the participation of the woman [in the process of substitution, so that if a woman makes a statement effecting an act of substitution, that statement is as valid as if a man had made it].

AA. That [view of his reading] is in accord with the following tradition assigned to Tannaitic authority:

BB. Since the entire formulation of the passage concerning an act of substitution speaks of the male, how in the end shall we encompass the female as well [so that an act of substitution of a woman is regarded as valid]?

CC. Scripture states, "And if changing, he shall change..."

DD. And as to rabbis, [how do they prove the same position]?

EE. It is from the use of the inclusionary word, *and*, in the phrase, "And if...."

FF. The usage, "And if...," in his view is not subject to exegesis at all [and yields no additional information about the role under discussion. Accordingly, in order to prove that a woman is involved in the process of substitution, as much as a man, Judah must refer solely to the intensive verb construction.]

What does 'All persons are obliged[5] to observe [the laws concerning] the booth' mean to include? – That is meant to include a minor that no more needs his mother,[6] for we have learnt: A minor that no more needs his mother is obliged to observe the laws concerning the booth.

[5]The Gemara proceeds now to a systematic examination of all cases in which the word 'all' is used. Unless it can be proved that in each case that word includes something normally excluded, the argument, or rather the first question posed on 2*a* will be invalidated.

[6]A child which (Suk. 28*b*) on awakening no more calls out 'Mother!' but attends to his needs, dresses himself, etc.

What does 'All are obliged to observe the law of the *lulab*'[8] mean to include? – That includes a minor who knows how to shake the *lulab*, for we learnt: A minor who knows how to shake[9] the *lulab* is obliged to observe [the laws of] the *lulab*. What

III. A. All are liable [to carry out the religious duty of dwelling in] a tabernacle [on the Festival of Tabernacles].

B. [When the framer of the foregoing statement makes explicit use of the inclusionary language, all], what [classification of persons is] encompassed, [that otherwise would have been omitted]?

C. It is to encompass a minor who does not depend upon his mother [but can take care of himself], in line with the following statement found in the Mishnah [M. Suk. 2:8]: *A child who does not depend upon his mother is liable to [carry out the religious duty of dwelling in a] tabernacle.*

D. All are liable [to carry out the religious duty of taking up] the palm branch [enjoined at Lev. 23:40.

E. [When the framer of the foregoing statement makes explicit use of the inclusionary language, all] what [classification of persons is] encompassed, [that otherwise would have been omitted]?

F. It is to encompass a minor

does 'All are obliged to observe the [law of] the fringes' include? – That includes the minor who knows how to wrap himself, for it was taught: A minor who knows how to wrap himself [into the *tallith*][10] is obliged to observe the law of the fringes. What does 'All are obliged to observe the rules concerning the *tefillin'* include? – That includes a minor who knows how to take care of the *tefillin*, for it was taught: If a minor knows how to take care of the *tefillin*,[11] his father buys *tefillin* for him.

[8]The palm branch forming with citron, myrtle and willow, the cluster taken during the Feast of Tabernacles (v. Lev. XIII, 40) is every day waved in every direction to symbolize the omnipresence of God.

[9]The *lulab* is waved in the four main directions: south, north, west, and east, and there are some details as to the position of the components of the cluster, which are known to the worshipper, so that he may follow the cantor's lead.

[10]The prayer shawl at the four corners of which the fringes are attached, and into which one wraps himself, 'in order to remember the commandments of the Lord'. The wrapping must be performed in a special manner, v. M.K. 24*a*.

[11]Commonly called phylacteries. The attachment, leather box and leather strap, each on left arm and forehead, containing the *Shema'* and other extracts from the Torah, originally worn all day, now only at the morning prayer.

who knows how to shake [the palm branch, so, with proper intention, making appropriate use of the holy object].

G. That is in line with the following statement found in the Mishnah [M. Suk. 3:15:] *A minor who knows how to shake [the palm branch with proper intention] is liable to [the religious duty of taking up] the palm branch.*

H. All are liable [to carry out the religious duty of affixing] fringes [to the corners of garments].

I. [When the framer of the foregoing statement makes explicit use of the inclusionary language, all] what [classification of persons is] encompassed, [that otherwise would have been omitted]?

J. It is to encompass a minor who knows how to cloak himself [in a garment, and so enters the obligation of affixing to said cloak the required fringes].

K. For it has been taught [in a teaching attributed to the authority of sages who occur in the Mishnah]: A minor who knows how to cloak himself [in a garment] is liable to [affix to that garment the required show] fringes.

L. All are liable [to carry out the religious duty of wearing] phylacteries.

M. [When the framer of the foregoing statement makes explicit use of the inclusionary language, all,] what [classification of persons is] encompassed, [that otherwise would have been omitted]?

N. It is to encompass a minor who knows how to take care of phylacteries [and therefore may be entrusted with them].

O. For it has been taught [in a teaching attributed to the authority of sages who occur in the Mishnah]: As to a minor who knows how to take care of phylacteries, his father purchases phylacteries for him.

What does 'All are obliged to appear' include[3] – It is meant to include one who is half[4] slave and half freedman. According, however, to Rabina, who holds that one who is half slave and half freed is free from the obligation to appear, [the word 'All'] is meant to include one who was lame[5] on the first day of the festival and became normal again on the second day. – That would be right according to the view that all the days of the festival may make up for each other. But according to the view that they all are but making up for the first day, what will 'All' come to include?[6] – It will include one blind in one of his eyes. This [answer] is not in accord with the following Tanna, for it was taught: Johanan b. Dahabai said in the name of R. Judah: One blind in one eye is free from the obligation to appear, for it is said:[7] *Yir'eh-yera'eh* [he shall see – he shall appear] i.e., just as He is present to see [the comer], so shall He be seen, just as His sight is complete, so shall the sight of him who appears be intact.

[3]Ex. XXIII, 17: *Three times in the year all thy males shall appear before the Lord God.* The scriptural text is all-inclusive, hence the mishnaic 'All' must deal with a case which, but for its redundant 'all', one would have excluded from the obligation to appear.

[4]A full slave is free because *'before the Lord God'* is interpreted to mean: only those who have but one Lord or Master, i.e., excluding the slave, who has a terrestrial master in addition to the Eternal Lord to serve. If owned by two masters, one of whom frees him, the slave becomes half freed, and stays half slave.

[5]The word *regel* in Hebrew may mean either *'foot'* or *'festival'* (on the three festivals the men *'footed'* it to Jerusalem). Hence the inference

IV. A. All are liable [on the occasion of a pilgrim festival to bring] an appearance-offering [to the Temple and to sacrifice it there in honor of the festival].

B. [When the framer of the foregoing statement makes explicit use of the inclusionary language, all,] what [classification of persons is] encompassed, [that otherwise would have been omitted]?

C. It is to encompass a person who is half slave and half free. [Such a person is subject to the stated liability of bringing an appearance-offering. But a person who is wholly a slave is exempt from the stated requirement of making the pilgrimage and bringing the offering.]

D. But in the view of Rabina, who has made the statement that one who is half slave and half free [also] is exempt from the obligation of bringing an appearance-offering [in celebration of the pilgrim festival], what [classification of persons] is encompassed [by the specification that all are subject to the stated obligation]?

E. It is to encompass a person who is lame on the first day of the festival but is restored [to full activity] on the second day. [A lame person is exempt from the religious obligation of coming up to Jerusalem on the pilgrim festival, since he obviously cannot make the trip. If, however, as of the second day of the festival, the lame person should be healed, then, according to the formulation of the rule at hand, such a person would become obligated, retroactively, to bring the required appearance-offering, as of the first day.]

F. [The foregoing statement rests on the position that on the successive days of the festival, one has the option of meeting an obligation incurred but not met on the earlier day. Thus if one did not make the that only those who could foot it normally are obliged to appear on these three festivals, which excludes a lame man.

[6]There are two views as to the statement of the Mishnah (Hag. 9a: One who has made no offering on the first day of the feast must make up, or has the opportunity to make up for it, throughout the other days of the festival), the first holding that each day has its own obligation; hence even if the worshipper was unfit on the first day of the festival, provided he is fit on the next, he is not exempt on the other days *per se* imposing the obligation, whilst the other considers only the first day imposing the obligation of an offering. Consequently, if he was disqualified on the first day, or free of that obligation, he would be exempt a complementary offering. The practical difference, in our case, would be this: One who on the first day of the festival had been lame, hence not obliged to offer the festal sacrifices, would be free according to the second view, but according to the first, would be obliged to make the offering on one of the subsequent days of the festival.

[7]The massoretic text *y-r-'-h* may be accentuated to read either *yir'eh* (he will see) or *yera'eh* (he will be seen). The first reading applied to the Lord, the second to the Israelite appearing before Him, would be thus interpreted: Just as the Lord sees him 'with two eyes' i.e., with undisturbed vision, so shall the worshipper be one appearing with both eyes intact, i.e., with undiminished sight. For an alternative rendering v. Hag., Sonc. ed., p. 3. n. 3. Or, if you like, say this: In truth it is meant to include one who is half slave and half freedman, and if the view of Rabina should appear as the difficulty, this is no difficulty either; the first view is in required appearance-offering on the first day, he is obligated for it but also may make up for it on the later days of the festival. The obligation for one day pertains to, but then may be made up, on the days following, thus, on day three for day two, on day four for day three, and the like. Accordingly, at E we maintain, first, that the person becomes obligated on the second day, and, second, that the obligation then is retroactive to the first. So he can make up what he owes. But the obligation to begin with likewise is retroactive. On day two he became obligated for an appearance-offering to cover day one. Accordingly, what we have just proposed] fully accords with the position of him who said that offerings made on] all [of the days of the festival] serve as a means of carrying out the obligations incurred on each one of them [as just now explained].

G. But in the view of him who says that all of the days of the festival [may serve to make up only for an obligation] incurred on the first day [of the festival alone, so that, first, one does not incur an obligation on a later day of the festival affecting what one owes for an earlier day of the festival, and so that, second, if one is not obligated to bring an appearance-offering on the first day of the festival, he is not obligated to bring such an offering to all, what category of persons] is encompassed [by use of the inclusionary language, all]?

H. It serves to encompass a person who is blind in one eye. [A person blind in both eyes is exempt from the appearance-offering on the pilgrim festival. One fully sighted, of course, is liable. The intermediate category then is dealt with in the stated formulation].

I. Now that view would not accord with the following teaching in accord with the former Mishnah, the second with the later Mishnah. For we learnt: One who is half slave and half freed man shall serve himself one day and his master the other – thus Beth Hillel. Said Beth Shammai to them: You took care of the interests of his master, but you have done nothing [thereby] on his behalf. For he is unable to marry either a female slave or free woman. Shall he do without marriage? But the world was created only for propagation of the species, as it is said: *He created it not a waste. He formed it to be inhabited.* Rather, for the sake of the social welfare we force his master to set him free, and the slave writes out a document of indebtedness covering the other half of his value. Beth Hillel retracted and taught as Beth Shammai.

the authority of sages of the Mishnah, as it has been taught:

J. Yohanan b. Dahabbai says in the name of R. Judah, "One who is blind in one eye is exempt from the religious duty of bringing an appearance-offering, for it is said, 'He will see... he will see...' (Ex. 23:14) [reading the scriptural language not as 'make an appearance,' but, with a shift in the vowels, 'will see'].

K. "[The proposed mode of reading the verse at hand yields the following consequence:] Just as one comes to see [the face of the Lord], so he comes to be seen. Just as one sees with two eyes, so one is seen with two eyes" [cf. T. Hag. 1:1F-H]. [The exegesis then excludes a person blind in one eye.]

L. If you prefer, [however, we may revert to the earlier proposal, and] state: Indeed, [the use of the inclusionary language is meant] to encompass a person who is half slave and half free.

M. And now as to the question you raised above, that that position would not accord with the opinion of Rabina, that indeed poses no problem.

N. [Why not?] The formulation at hand, [which prohibits the half-slave half-free man from bringing the necessary offering] is in line with the original formulation of the Mishnah-law [prior to the debate, cited presently, between the Houses of Shammai and Hillel]. The other formulation [which permits and hence requires the half-slave half-free person, in the intermediate status, to bring the appearance-offering] is in line with the posterior formulation of the Mishnah-law.

O. For we have learned [at M. Git. 4:5:]

P. *"He who is half-slave and half-free works for his master one day and for himself one day," the words of the House of Hillel.*

Q. *Said to them the House of*

*Shammai, "You have taken good care of his master, but of himself you have not taken care.*

R. *"To marry a slave-girl is not possible, for half of him after all is free.*

S. *"[To marry] a free woman is not possible, for half of him after all is a slave.*

T. *"Shall he refrain?*

U. *"But was not the world made only for procreation, as it is said, 'He created it not a waste, he formed it to be inhabited' (Is. 45:18).*

V. *"But: For the good order of the world,"they force his master to free him.*

W. *"And he [the slave] writes him a bond covering half his value."*

X. *And the House of Hillel reverted to teach in accord with the opinion of the House of Shammai.* [Accordingly, the law prior to the reversion specified at X treated one who is half slave and half free as in a fixed category, and such a one would not bring an appearance-offering, since he was partially a slave. But after the reversion, one who was half slave and half free could leave that interstitial category easily and so would not be regarded as essentially a slave. Such a one then would be obligated to bring the appearance-offering, there being no permanent lord over him except for the Lord God.]

What does 'All are obliged to sound the *shofar*' mean to include? – That includes a minor who has reached the age of training, for we learnt: One does not prevent a minor from blowing the *shofar* on the festival.[1]

[1] R.H. 32b. The source quoted does not seem to fit the inference made, for the answer postulates evidence that a minor is obliged to sound the *shofar*, whereas the reference quoted refers to the fact

V. A. All are obligated [to the religious duty of hearing] the sounding of the ram's horn [on the New Year].

B. [When the framer of the passage makes use of the inclusionary language, all,] what [classification of persons does he thereby] encompass?

C. It is to encompass a minor who has reached the age [at which he is able to benefit from] instruction.

D. For we have learned [in a

that one does not prevent a minor from sounding the horn, which allows for the possibility of his being neither obliged nor forbidden to sound it. There is a lacuna in the text which Tosaf. s.v. *'yn m$^c$kbyn* supplies, from R.H. 33a, where such obligation is definitely stated.

teaching attributed to the authority of Mishnah-sages:] They do not prevent a minor from sounding the ram's horn on the festival day.

'All are obliged to read the scroll. All are fit to read the scroll.' What are these meant to include? – [3a] They are meant to include women, in accord with the view of R. Joshua b. Levi; for R. Joshua b. Levi said: Women are obliged to read the scroll because they too, had a part in that miracle.[1] What does 'All are obliged to arrange *zimmun*[2] mean to include? – It means to include women and slaves, for it was taught: Women are under the obligation of *zimmun* amongst themselves, and slaves are under the obligation of *zimmun* amongst themselves. What does 'All may be joined to a *zimmun*' mean to include? – That includes a minor who knows to Whom one pronounces a blessing. What does 'All defile by reason of their flux' include? – That includes a child one day old, for it was taught: [It could have said,] *When a man [hath an issue out of his flesh].'* Why does the text state 'any man'? That is to include a child one day old, [teaching] that he defiles by reason of his flux; this is the view of R. Judah. R. Ishmael the son of R. Johanan b. Beroka says: [This inference] is not necessary, for behold, Scripture reads: *And of them that have an issue whether it be a male or a female,* i.e., once he is *'a male,'* however minor or major, once she is *'a female,'* whether minor or major. If so, why does the Torah use [the redundant phrase] *'any man'*? The Torah speaks in the language of man.[3]

VI. A. All are subject to the religious obligation of hearing the reading of the Scroll of Esther.

B. All are suitable to read the Scroll of Esther aloud [for the community, thereby fulfilling the religious obligation of all those who are present].

C. [When the framer of the passage makes use of the inclusionary language, all,] what [classification of persons does he thereby] encompass [3A]?

D. It is to encompass women [who may read the Scroll of Esther aloud for the community and thereby carry out the obligation of all present to do so].

E. This view accords with the position of R. Joshua b. Levi. For R. Joshua b. Levi said, "Women are liable [to the religious duty of] the reading of the Scroll of Esther, for they too were included in the miracle [of redemption from Israel's enemies, celebrated on Purim]."

VII. A. All are liable to the religious duty of saying Grace in public quorum [if they have eaten together. They thus may not say Grace after meals by themselves, if a quorum of three persons is present. In that circumstance a public recitation, involving a call to Grace, is required.]

B. [When the framer of the rule uses the inclusionary word, all,] what [classification of persons does he mean to] include?

C. He means to encompass women and slaves.

[1]V. Meg. 4a, Rashi and Tosaf. Either they too were included in Haman's decree of extinction, or their merit, too, brought about the miracle of the deliverance.

[2]Ber. 45a: Three who ate together are under the obligation of *zimmun*, i.e. of saying grace together. Literally *zimmun* means appointing and may thus refer to the appointment to eat together, with the implied obligation to say grace together.

[3]The repetition of the word *'man'* is redundant. *'Ish ish'* means every man, any man.

D. For it has been taught [in a teaching bearing the authority of Mishnah-teachers:] Women say Grace in public as a group [unto] themselves, and slaves do likewise. [Accordingly, both classifications of persons are subject to the liability of saying a public Grace, should a quorum of appropriate persons be present].

VIII. A. All join in the public saying of Grace [responding to the call to say Grace].

B. [When the framer of the ruler uses the cited inclusionary language,] what [classification of persons] does he mean to encompass?

C. It is to encompass a minor who has knowledge on his own concerning Him to whom they say a blessing [in the Grace after meals].

D. That is in line with what R. Nahman said, "He who knows to Whom they say a blessing [in the Grace after meals] – they encompass such a one in the public call to say the Grace after meals."

IX. A. All are subject to becoming unclean by reason of the flux [specified at Lev. 15:1ff.].

B. [When the framer of the rule uses the cited inclusionary language,] what [classification of persons does he mean to] encompass?

C. It is to encompass an infant one day old [who, should he produce a flux, would be deemed subject to flux-uncleanness under appropriate circumstances. This form of genital uncleanness is not limited to an adult.]

D. For it has been taught [in a teaching bearing the authority of Mishnah-sages:] "'[When any] man [produces flux out of his flesh]' (Lev. 15:2).

E. "Now why does the Author of Scripture state, 'When any man...' [so indicating an inclusion of some category beyond man]?

F. "It is to encompass even an infant a day old, who thus is subject to the uncleanness of flux," the words of R. Judah.

G. R. Ishmael, the son of R. Yohanan b. Beroqah, says, "It is hardly necessary [to interpret Scripture in such wise]. Lo, [Scripture] says, 'And any of them who has an issue, whether it is male or female' (Lev. 15:33).

H. "[The sense is], 'Male,' meaning, whoever is male, whether minor or adult. 'Female' [means], whoever is female, whether minor or adult. [Both categories, minor and adult, male and female, fall within the classification of those subject to uncleanness through flux. Scripture is explicit in this matter, without the necessity of interpreting the language important in Judah's view.]

I. "If that is the case, then on what account does [the Author of Scripture] use the language, 'If any man...'? [The Author of] the Torah made use of the language of common speech [and did not mean to provide occasions for exegesis of minor details of formulation]."

Let me conclude by stating why I think the present approach improves upon the former one. In my view the work of transmitting an ancient text to a new generation should go on so long as new readers in successive ages come to the classic document. No great text of antiquity has ever reached English only one time, and then for all time. As I said in the opening discussion, just as one generation after another has taken up the challenge of translating and therefore interpreting Plato and Aristotle, Euripides and Herodotus, not to mention the Hebrew Scriptures and the New Testament, so the classics of Judaism, the Mishnah, the Tosefta, the several scriptural-exegetical compilations ("midrashim"), the Talmud of the Land of Israel, and the Talmud of Babylonia demand renewed encounter in each succeeding age. The reason is not solely the possibility that a better text, better lexicographical aids, better interpretative commentaries, become available. In the case of Bavli, that presently is certainly not the case.

It is that a new generation simply raises a fresh set of questions and so wants a translation that addresses its concerns in particular.

In my case and in that of my colleagues at work on the other tractates of the Talmud of Babylonia, we come with all due respect for the achievements of our predecessors. If in any aspect we improve upon their work, the reason is that, to begin with, we build upon what they already have achieved. What we want to know, which the Soncino generation did not, is several things. First, how the materials of the Bavli fall into diverse genres; second, how the framers of the document arranged their discussion of the Mishnah; third, what sorts of materials, in addition to those serving as Mishnah-exegesis, they constructed or borrowed; and fourth, how they proposed to put the whole together.

In other words, apart from occasional improvements in the understanding of a passage, though we would not claim that that is common, our principal contribution lies in the more analytical character of our translation than that which came before. We do not present long columns of undifferentiated type, broken up merely by paragraphs. We distinguish from one another the large-scale and complete discussions of problems or topics. Within these large-scale discussions we distinguish one completed thought from another. In our remarks at the end of each of the discussions of a Mishnah-paragraph, we furthermore comment on the relationship to the Mishnah-paragraph at hand of the completed units of thought of the Bavli.

For the reader who does not know Hebrew and Aramaic at all, we add an enormous quantity of explanatory language, included in square brackets in the text, to make the text readable and accessible in its own terms. The footnotes of the Soncino translators simply do not lead a reader through the text. In most instances, the Soncino translators take for granted a fundamental comprehension of the text in Aramaic that, if widely present, would have rendered the work of translation superfluous to begin with. To put matters more bluntly, where the text is not self-evidently accessible, the Soncino translators do not seem to make it so. My principal contribution is to attempt to remedy this enormous failing in the otherwise superb work of those who attempted the work before now.

We readily add our hope that those who in a coming generation will undertake yet another translation will improve upon what we have done. So, in all, successive ages will call forth translators who aim at making clear and readily understood in the host-language what hithertofore has been puzzling and essentially incomprehensible (however elegantly worded). In all, therefore, we do not apologize to our predecessors in the ongoing work of translating the great text at hand, while we also do not for one minute denigrate their contribution. We recognize the abiding value of what they did, and we hope that for another age we may improve upon what is now available.

It goes without saying, moreover, that as scholarship in the Bavli's Aramaic becomes accessible in dictionaries, as study of the text and exegesis of its meanings reaches still higher levels, and as a critical edition and commentary come to realization, translators will bring to the text at hand a still deeper grasp of its meanings than we do. We should label this translation "preliminary," if it were not so evident to us that any translation of the Talmud of Babylonia at this primitive stage in our knowledge must be preliminary. We work on translation before the completion of a critical text, a competent dictionary, and a reliable commentary drawing upon the exegetical achievements of all times. On that basis, any translation must be regarded as temporary and, at best, a mere expedient. But even under better circumstances, with good dictionaries and reliable Hebrew texts, for instance, we should take for granted that those who follow us will wish to retranslate the same texts on which we have worked. That is the way, the only way, in which they shall make their own what is the heritage of all ages.

# 3

# Translation as Conversation: A Specimen of the Palestinian Talmud in English

## Yerushalmi Sotah 5:2

The Mishnah is a highly formalized document, so that, in translation, we must pay very close attention to word order and persistent word choice, but the Palestinian Talmud presents us with a quite different kind of text and hence a totally unprecedented problem of translation. The difference may be expressed very simply. If we translate the Mishnah literally, word for word, we get in American English an essentially comprehensible sentence, requiring little or no gloss (other than facts) to produce nearly complete intelligibility. If we translate a passage of the Palestinian Talmud word for word, without elaborate and protracted insertions of materials, what we generally get is pure gibberish. The Mishnah is meant to be understood within the limitation of its own language. Its meaning is conveyed (apart from facts required for making sense of the document, and apart from the facts of Scripture in particular) essentially through the way the Mishnah's framers construct their sentences and lay out their formal and formulary patterns. The Palestinian Talmud is a totally different sort of writing.

It is premature to speculate on the literary theory behind the use of language in the Palestinian Talmud. Until the entire document has been rendered into some language other than the original (and modern Hebrew would be at least as suitable for this purpose as American English), we can say nothing of a systematic and careful nature about its modes of thought and expression and their special and institutional purposes. All we can do, until the entire work is before us, is guess. We at best contribute examples without a clear notion of how much of the whole, or how little, they actually exemplify. But it is not premature to give some picture of what it takes to translate a long and difficult passage of the Palestinian Talmud into English. On the contrary, by presenting this sample, I hope to elicit the comments and suggestions of colleagues.

The single significant trait in what follows is the extensive use of square brackets to add to the flow of discourse those sources alluded to but not cited. The translation is richly augmented by understanding not made explicit and by rhetorical shifts and turns in no way indicated in the original Aramaic. To state the theory of translation of this document as simply as I can: Here I propose to talk my way through an account of what the document says – not stated in square brackets but translated into fairly fluent American English – and of what the document means. That is, both what we need to know to make sense of it, and also what we are supposed to conclude on the basis of what the document says and the facts added by us, are supplied.

Translation here is a kind of extended conversation, an interchange within the document, with the document, and through the document. Clearly, this is a different theory indeed from that governing the way the Mishnah should be translated. A good translation of the Mishnah, as I said, is virtually literal, with a minimum of intruded language or inserted ideas, facts, and problems. The difference is based upon the utterly unrelated literary traits of the two documents. The Mishnah is to Scripture as is Yerushalmi to it. As indifferent as is the Mishnah, supposed to be "Oral Torah," to the literary and linguistic traits of the Mosaic Revelation, the Written Torah, so indifferent are the framers of the Palestinian Talmud to the literary and linguistic traits of the Mishnah.

Nor can it be supposed that the Palestinian Talmud is (merely) a commentary to the Mishnah. Unless by "commentary" we mean something more like an encyclopaedia of relevant or intersecting materials, together with a vast and independent philosophical treatise, along with a sustained exercise in practical reason and applied logic, the Palestinian Talmud is not a commentary in any sense. More often than not, the Mishnah presents little more than a topic for Yerushalmi's quite free-ranging and independent treatment. Consequently, we cannot explain the elliptical and crabbed "style" (if it can be called a style at all) through which the Palestinian Talmud expresses its ideas. Nor are we able to make sense of Yerushalmi's recurrent, therefore deliberate, rhetoric by reference to the literary tasks facing its framers.

If I had to make a guess as to what we have, I should imagine we deal with nothing more than brief notes, notations really, out of which a whole and complete discourse is supposed to be reconstructed by those essentially familiar with the (original) discourse. Yerushalmi is a kind of abbreviated script, a set of cue cards drastically cut down to a minimum of words. But these metaphors are meant only to account for the theory of translation followed here. I mean the theory that out of the sherds and remnants of coherent speech we have to reconstruct and fully reconstitute the (original) coherent discourse, as best we can. Whole sentences from key words, whole analyses from truncated allusions.

In the case of a document that assumes so vast a knowledge of the Hebrew Scriptures and the Mishnah as does the Palestinian Talmud, even if one quotes the whole of a verse alluded to only by a word or two, should the translator then proceed to interpret that verse? Its context? Its meaning and use in the passage of the Talmud before us?

Similarly, if the Talmud rests upon a pericope of the Mishnah that is not cited at all, should the translator merely allude to the passage and expect the reader to look it up? Should the translator cite the passage in full? And if so, how extensive an explanation is required?

Third, as to the discourse of the Talmud itself, the translation, of course, constitutes a substantial judgment upon the meaning of the text. Where we put a period or a comma, or indicate the end of one major discourse and the start of another, how we break up the undifferentiated columns of words into paragraphs, the paragraphs into sentences, and the sentences into their individual, small units of cognition – these decisions are conveyed in the very simple facts of how we present what we claim to be the meaning of the text. And yet, beyond that simple statement, it is clear, a fair amount of explanation is demanded.

How much, or how little, must be explained is not self-evident, and probably will never be readily settled. It is invariably an exercise of judgment and taste. That is why, as I said, the translator has to find a balance between the requirements of intelligibility, indeed, to whom it may concern, on the one side, and the limited possibilities of full and ample presentation of a single text in a single book, on the other. Too much will overwhelm the reader, who will lose sight of the text, which is, after all, at the center of the translation. Too little will puzzle the reader, leaving the text translated but still inaccessible.

Only a reference translation, putting down on paper only the corresponding words in the other language so that people may look things up and pick and choose what may be useful, justifies an essentially unadorned translation, a simple "rendition" from one language to the other.

A research translation meant to raise and solve all the problems, philological and linguistic, textual and lexicographical, historical and theological, ranging here, there, and everywhere, with endless notes and a dazzling display of erudition – such a translation seems to me of equally limited use. For someone opening it will find overwhelming the limitless ranges of erudite discourse and so lose sight of the issue at hand. That issue is the protracted and brilliant exercise in practical reason and applied logic which is the Palestinian Talmud at its most interesting, if also its most difficult.

The sample before the reader is meant to be something in between a reference translation and a research translation. It is, perhaps inaptly, to be called a conversation translation, a "talking-of-one's-way-through-the-text." It should be self-evident that the translator undertook the project for a purpose other than the need, not widely expressed, for an American-English version of the Palestinian Talmud. It is to make possible an entirely separate set of historical and religious studies of the Judaism represented by the Palestinian Talmud. Accordingly, the focus here is upon the meaning of the text. The special interest is in a clear and careful account of what is said. The reference translation I deem inadequate, because it is essentially useless, in leaving the text unexplained. The research translation has merit since it stands as a convenient source for whatever is relevant (and much that is not relevant) to the particular text subject to translation. But it is not a great deal more useful than the reference translation for those whose principal interest is in what this text says and what it means. This conversation translation then serves a very particular purpose. It is addressed to a reader of a singular sort, who wants to make some sense of this important document for Judaism of late antiquity, so as to understand that Judaism.

In the translation that follows, the Mishnah is given in italics, and when it is cited, it is cited in italics. That supplies a clear visual picture of the relationship of the Talmud to the Mishnah. When Tosefta is cited, it is given in bold face, so that its place in the document also is highlighted. The text is broken up into complete units of discourse – eight in all – and each unit of discourse is broken up into its constituent paragraphs, each paragraph one complete thought, if not an entire sentence. For ease of reference, each unit of thought is marked by a letter.

*Yerushalmi Sotah 5:2*

**Mishnah Sotah 5:2**

A. *On that day did R. 'Aqiba expound as follows: "'And every earthen vessel whereinto any of them falls, whatsoever is in it conveys uncleanness'* (Lev. 11:33).
*"It does not say 'It will be unclean,' but 'will convey uncleanness' – that is to impart uncleanness to other things.*

B. *"Thus the Scripture taught concerning a loaf of bread unclean in the second remove, that it imparts uncleanness in the third remove [to a loaf of bread with which it comes into contact]."*

C. *Said R. Joshua, "Who will remove the dirt from your eyes, Rabban Yoḥanan b. Zakkai, for you used to say, 'Another generation is going to come to declare clean a loaf of bread in the third remove' [from the original source of uncleanness].*

D. *"For there is no Scripture in the Torah which indicates that it is unclean.*

E. *"But now has not 'Aqiba, your disciple, brought scriptural proof from the Torah that it is indeed unclean,*

F. *since it is said, 'And whatsoever is in it shall impart uncleanness'* (Lev. 11:33).

**I.**

A. [With regard to 'Aqiba's view that a loaf of bread unclean in the second remove from the original source of uncleanness has the capacity to impart uncleanness to food with which it comes into contact, hence at the third remove from the original source of uncleanness, R. Yosé b. R. Bun said, "Rab and Samuel disputed about this matter.]

B. "One of them said, 'Whether the food is in the status of heave-offering [and hence, both more sensitive to becoming unclean, and also more capable of imparting uncleanness], or in the status of unconsecrated food, R. 'Aqiba's opinion applies.'

C. "The other of them said, 'If the food is in the status of heave-offering, R. 'Aqiba's opinion applies, but food [unclean in the second remove] which is not consecrated [does] not [have the power to impart uncleanness to food with which it comes into contact. Hence there is no third remove in the matter of unconsecrated food's contracting uncleanness. Unconsecrated food in the third remove from the original source of uncleanness itself is completely clean and does not receive uncleanness from food in the second remove from the original source of uncleanness.]'

D. "Now we do not know which one of them held one opinion, and which one held the other.

E. "But on the basis of that which R. Yosé in the name of R. Jonah, and some say that Rab said it in the name of R. Hiyya the Great, namely, 'What is unclean in the third remove from the original source is unclean because of the effects of the dead creeping thing,' [which was that original source, and that is stated without differentiation as to the character of the food – unconsecrated, consecrated – which receives the uncleanness], it follows that it is he who has said that R. 'Aqiba's position applies both to heave-offering and to unconsecrated food alike."

F. [Now that we have established the grounds for dispute, we turn to other laws of Mishnah to test the more controversial of the two positions, namely, Rab's.] The Mishnah-pericope which follows stands at variance with the position of Rab:

G. *Produce a tithe which was rendered susceptible to uncleanness by liquid and which a Tebul Yom [one who has immersed and who now awaits sunset to complete the process of complete purification from uncleanness] touched, or [which] dirty hands [touched, which are unclean in the second remove] – they separate from that produce in the status of tithe heave-offering of tithe in a state of uncleanness [and said heave-offering is clean], because it is in the third remove, and the third remove from the original source of uncleanness is clean so far as unconsecrated food is concerned* (M. T.Y. 4:1). [So there is no status of uncleanness imputed to food which is not consecrated and which suffers contact with food unclean in the second remove. Surely 'Aqiba has been misinterpreted by Rab, or 'Aqiba must differ from the cited pericope.]

H. Interpret the passage as a lenient ruling in regard to uncleanness affecting the hands, since the perpetual uncleanness of the hands [in the second remove] is merely by reason of a decree of the scribes.

I. And lo, we have learned, *A Tebul Yom* [so it cannot be a leniency accorded only to the hands]!

J. Interpret the rule to apply to a Tebul Yom who has immersed himself by reason of the doubtful uncleanness imparted by being in a grave-area [which may or may not contain corpse matter sufficient to impart uncleanness. Since we do not know for sure that the person was originally made unclean by a corpse, we also have no reason to impose the full stringencies of the law,hence the stated leniency as to food in the third remove from the original source of uncleanness. But in general, there is indeed a third remove of uncleanness affecting ordinary, not consecrated, food.]

K. Said R. Zeira, "[There is a still better solution]. Even if you say that the Tebul Yom under discussion is unclean by reason of an uncleanness specified by the Torah, the case of the Tebul Yom still is different. He is described in Scripture as both clean and unclean. He is clean so far as unconsecrated food is concerned even while it is yet day, and he is clean for heave-offering only after the sun has set."

L. R. Haggai objected before R. Yosé, "[There is an alternative explanation for the usage of the words, 'unclean' and 'clean,' with regard to the Tebul Yom.] One may say that [the entire passage speaks only of food in the status of heave-offering, and] the Tebul Yom [during the day before the sun set] is clean so far as touching the consecrated food is concerned, but unclean [until sunset] so far as eating it is concerned."

M. He said to him, "The cited passage (Lev. 11:33) refers explicitly to utensils. Have you got the possibility of maintaining that, with respect to utensils, they may be clean so far as being touched is concerned and unclean so far as being eaten in concerned?!"

N. The Mishnah pericope now cited also supports the position of Rab:
*Unconsecrated food in the first remove from the original source of uncleanness is unclean and imparts uncleanness [to food which it touches]. Unconsecrated food in the second remove is unfit [to be eaten by one who eats his unconsecrated food in cleanness] but does not impart uncleanness at all. And unconsecrated food in the third remove [that is, which has touched unconsecrated food unclean in the second remove] may be eaten in a pottage of heave-offering* (M. Toh. 2:3). [This is the view of Rab, that 'Aqiba's view is that there is a third remove to be taken into consideration for both heave-offering and unconsecrated food. Why?]

O. Now lo, it is prohibited to mix food in the third remove with heave-offering [and hence there is indeed a consideration of uncleanness affecting unconsecrated food in the third remove. If there is no such consideration, one may not mix the unconsecrated food in the third remove with heave-offering?]

P. [Now, this is not possible. For] cite what follows: *Heave-offering in the first and in the second removes is unclean and renders other food unclean. Heave-offering in the third remove is unfit and does not convey uncleanness. And heave-offering at the fourth remove is eaten in a pottage of Holy Things* (M. Toh. 2:4). [Thus what is unclean at the third remove invalidates what it touches at the fourth, but it does not render it unclean so that what is at the fourth remove has an affect upon what it touches, that is, at the fifth remove.]

Q. Now if you reason as you did above, then it must follow that it is forbidden to treat what is unclean in the fourth remove as holy. Then you turn out to impute to Rab contradictory positions.

R. For R. Ba in the name of Rab [stated], "What is unclean in the third remove is affected by the original dead creeping thing's uncleanness. But as to what is affected in the fourth remove, it is indeed permitted to treat it as holy [and it is not unclean at all].

S. "For the consideration of a fourth remove from the original source as uncleanness affects Holy Things only so far as the Most Holy Things of the sanctuary itself are concerned. [Hence the implication drawn just now contradicts Rab's position in the present matter.]"

T. Said R. Huna, "And are we not speaking here of heave-offering [and not of Holy Things]? And as to heave-offering, it is prohibited to treat it as subject to the laws governing Holy Things [which are more severe], so as not to cause any sort of mishandling of food in the status of heave-offering. [Since the rules are less strict, if one treats heave-offering by a more strict rule than is required, one will end up disposing of it, instead of eating it, when in fact it is valid and may be eaten. So there is no contradiction among Rab's several opinions.]

U. And, further, cite what follows: *Holy Things in the first, second, and third removes are susceptible to uncleanness and impart uncleanness. Holy Things in the fourth remove are unfit and do not impart uncleanness. And Holy Things in the fifth remove are eaten in a pottage of Holy Things* (M. Toh. 2:5).

V. Now if you say this, then it is forbidden to treat as holy what has touched what is unclean in the fourth remove. [It cannot be eaten by itself.]

W. Now is there such a thing as the consideration of a fifth remove from the original source of uncleanness so far as Holy Things are concerned? [Certainly not.]

X. [It follows that the original, acute reading of the pericope vis-à-vis Rab is not possible. For] you must rule that there is no such thing [as a fifth remove in Holy Things], and here too there is no such thing as a third remove, as reasoned above, N-Q. The entire argument is thus shown to lead to an absurd extreme and must be dropped.

**II.**

A. [That which has touched something unclean in the second remove is clean, for, in line with Lev. 11:33,] said R. Yohanan, "That which is in the third remove is third in contact with the dead creeping thing, [and it is not unclean, so] it is permitted to treat it as heave-offering [that is, to declare that batch of food as heave-offering for some larger batch of clean food. There is nothing unclean about it.]"

B. They asked before him: "[Is this statement of yours] even in accord with R. 'Aqiba (at M. 5:2B)?"

C. R. Yosé in the name of R. Hila, "And it even accords with the position of R. 'Aqiba." [Yosé-Hila maintain the position of Samuel, that at issue in 'Aqiba's saying is only food in the status of heave-offering.]

D. "How so?"

E. "A Tebul Yom is invalid [for eating heave-offering, since he is in the second remove], and that which is in the second remove is invalid [for use as heave-offering. That is, invalid but not unclean.]

F. "Just as a Tebul Yom does not invalidate unconsecrated food touched by him from being declared heave-offering [for he does not impart uncleanness to that which he touches],

G. "so [whatever is] in the second remove [like the Tebul Yom] does not invalidate unconsecrated food [by rendering it unclean] from being declared heave-offering."

H. [Taking the opposite line of thought, that 'Aqiba treats unconsecrated food as much as heave-offering], R. Yosé in the name of R. Yohanan: "That which is unclean in the third remove is unclean by reason of the contact with the dead creeping thing [as much as that which is in the second remove from the original contact]. Consequently, it is permitted to declare food unclean in the third remove to be heave-offering. It is [still] forbidden to treat it as Holy Things [for, in the case of other food in the status of Holy Things it will impart uncleanness and so render such food invalid. But the uncleanness, so far as heave-offering is concerned, is imparted by food in the second remove to food in the third remove, at which point the process ends for heave-offering. The net effect is to extend the process for heave-offering into the third remove, rather than into the second remove, as is the case of unconsecrated food. This is in line with Rab's view of 'Aqiba's meaning.]"

I. R. Zeira raised the following question before R. Yosé, "It imparts uncleanness to food in the status of Holy Things, and do you say this? [If the heave-offering in the third remove can impart uncleanness to food in the status of Holy Things, then how can you deem it clean when it is in the third remove? Why stop here?]"

J. He said to him, "It is because of the more strict procedures attendant upon food in the status of Holy Things."

K. Said R. Samuel bar R. Isaac, "The essence of the uncleanness imputed to food in the status of Holy Things is [merely] by reason of the more strict procedures attendant upon food in that status. [That is, to protect such food in that status, uncleanness is imputed at a further remove from the original source of uncleanness than the law would ordinarily require]."

L. [Along these same lines] said R. Yosé, "And why does it impart uncleanness in the case of Holy Things? Because of the more strict procedures attendant upon food in the status of Holy Things [=I-J]."

M. [Reverting to the issue of the relationship of food in the status of Holy Things to unconsecrated food, in which contact with food unclean in the second remove leaves said food (that is, in the third remove) clean, said R. Yudan, "And even in accord with rabbis, who maintain that there is no consideration of uncleanness at the third remove in the case of unconsecrated food, why is it said that such food [that is, in the third remove] imparts uncleanness in the case of food in the status of Holy Things [as at M. Toh. 2:2-4]? It is again because of the more strict procedures attendant upon food in the status of Holy Things."

N. Said to him R. Yosé, "And do we really need to hear a teaching along this line from a great man such as yourself? [Yosé is of the view that ordinary food which is prepared by the rules governing preservation of the cleanness of Holy Things remains in its status as ordinary food. It does not enter the status of food in the status of Holy Things. Accordingly, the very consideration introduced at M is irrelevant to all potential circumstances. That is, there cannot be a case in which unconsecrated food in the third remove affects food in the status of Holy Things and so invalidates it. For all such food in any case will be deemed null, clean to begin with, since unconsecrated food leaves the ladder of uncleanness in the third and fourth removes from the original source of contamination.]"

**III.**

A. [With reference to M. 5:2, Joshua's statement], there [in Babylonia] they say, "Since R. Joshua praised R. 'Aqiba, that is to say that the practiced law accords with ['Aqiba's] position."

B. Rabbis of Caesarea say, "He praised him for his exegetical achievement. But for all practical purposes the law does not accord with his position."

**IV.**

A. For R. Aha, R. Miasha in the name of R. Eleazar said, "Flogging is not administered to one [who brings] tithe [into contact with food unclean in the second remove from the original source of uncleanness] and so puts it into the third remove [from that original source.] And even in accord with the view of R. 'Aqiba, flogging is not administered. [There is no consideration of a third remove from the original source of uncleanness, either for ordinary food or for tithe. One who is supposed to eat his food in a state of cleanness – whether tithe or unconsecrated food – hence will not be flogged for eating food in the third remove from the original source.]"

B. Why should this be so?

C. A Tebul Yom has the power of invalidation [and he is in the status of that which in a second remove from the original source of uncleanness],

D. and that which is in the second remove invalidates.

E. Just as a Tebul Yom who is in contact with unconsecrated food has no effect upon it [in that the food need not await sunset to be deemed clean again (PM)],

F. so that which is unclean in the second remove which is in contact with unconsecrated food has no effect upon it.

G. Said R. Eleazar, "As we count removes of uncleanness in the case of unconsecrated food, so we count removes of uncleanness in the case of tithe [as has just now been illustrated at C-F]."

H. This is in line with that which R. Jonah, R. Imi said in the name of R. Simeon b. Laqish, "In all other circumstances we deal with unconsecrated food, but in the present context we deal with tithe [and that indicates, as Eleazar has just said, that the two are subject to a single set of rules]."

I. Said R. Yosé, "And even with regard to [second tithe] which is unclean in the first remove [from the original source of uncleanness] is not so clearly prohibited. If someone eats second tithe in the first remove, it is not so obvious that he should be flogged. Why not?

J. ["I have not eaten of the tithe while I was mourning or removed any of it while I was unclean" (Deut. 26:14)]. "'I shall not eat...,' is not written, but rather, 'I *did* not eat...,' [and, as we shall now see, the difference matters]."

K. Said R. Abba Meri, "How do we know [that the statement before us is not deemed a negative commandment at all, on account of which one may be flogged]? For it is written, '...according to all that thou hast commanded me' (Deut. 26:14), as if it were not entirely clear. [That is to say, the confession states that one will not have kept the commandment in its proper way if he eats the second tithe in a state of uncleanness. But there is no negative commandment in that regard. It is simply part of the general advice on how to do things right, and for violating such instructions one is not flogged.]"

V.

A. R. Abbahu in the name of R. Mana, "On what account did they rule 'Unconsecrated food which is unclean in the second remove imparts uncleanness to unconsecrated liquids'? [For we know full well that unconsecrated food in the second remove does not impart uncleanness to unconsecrated solid food in the second remove at all. Yet in the case of liquids, the unconsecrated solids in the second remove have that very effect; indeed, the liquid then is deemed unclean in the *first* remove (cf. M. Toh. 2:2 ff.)].

B. "It is on account of the hands, which are deemed unclean in the second remove by decree of the scribes. They do impart uncleanness to unconsecrated liquid [putting the liquid into the first remove].

C. "[If that is so], then that which is unconsecrated in the second remove in accord with the teaching of the Torah [that is, in line with 'Aqiba's reading of Lev. 11:33, any unconsecrated food in the second remove], all the more so should have that same power to impart uncleanness to unconsecrated solid food in the second remove!"

D. "[What follows assumes knowledge of M. Toh. 4:7D-J, as follows: *A doubt concerning liquids, in respect to contracting uncleanness – it is deemed unclean. A doubt concerning liquids, in respect to conveying uncleanness – it is deemed clean. A doubt concerning hands, either in respect to contracting uncleanness or in respect to conveying uncleanness, or in respect to being made clean – [in all these cases matters of doubt are resolved as] clean.* Along these same lines, in accord with the proposition just now stated], just as in the case of uncleanness imparted by the hands, a matter of doubt as to whether the hands have imparted uncleanness to other things is deemed to be clean,

E. "so in the case of that which is unclean in the second remove [in general, as distinct from the hands], a doubt involving whether that which is unclean in the second remove has imparted uncleanness to other things is resolved as clean."

F. R. Hanina objected to R. Mana, "Lo, if one eats unclean food and drinks unclean liquid, a matter of doubt concerning them which affects their having imparted uncleanness to other things is resolved as unclean. [This is a strict rule, in that a doubt concerning their secondary effects is resolved in a strict way. If we do not know, for instance, that the person who ate or drank these unclean things touched an object, we assume that he has.]

G. "And as to liquids which exude from them, a matter of doubt affecting them, as to whether or not they have imparted uncleanness to other things, likewise is resolved as unclean. [Accordingly, in all these areas of doubt, which affect uncleanness imputed solely by decree of the scribes, we resolve doubt in a strict way.]

H. "And yet, that which is unclean in the second remove, which is a status imputed by the Torah and not merely by scribes [in line with 'Aqiba's exegesis] – should a matter of doubt affecting it so far as it has imparted uncleanness to other things be deemed clean? [Surely not!]"

I. Said R. Mana before R. Haninah, "And are we not in fact dealing with heave-offering [to which a more strict rule applies, and that accounts for the stringency outlined at F-H. But in the case of unconsecrated food, the lenient rule proposed by me, Mana, applies.]"

J. Said to him R. Hanina, "And even if you maintain that we are dealing with heave-offering, what difference does it make?

K. "'It will be unclean...it will convey uncleanness' represents the teaching of Torah (cf. M. 5:2A) [for liquid. The power of liquid to impart uncleanness to food is based on the law of the Torah.] Is that not [Yosé's view, in line with] 'Aqiba? [But *we* hold that the reference to uncleanness is to their *being* unclean, not to their *imparting* uncleanness. So the Torah-law is not involved. Consequently, the original question which I phrased at F-H indeed is valid. (For further discussion, cf. PM.)]"

**VI.**

A. There they have said [with reference to Haggai 2:11-14: "Thus says the Lord of hosts: Ask the priests to decide this question, 'If one carries holy flesh with the skirt of his garment and touches with his skirt bread, pottage, wine, oil, or any kind of food [in sequence], does it become holy?' The priests answered, 'No.' Then said Haggai, 'If one who is unclean by contact with a dead body touches any of these, does it become unclean?' The priests answered, 'It does become unclean.' Then Haggai said, 'So is it with this people...says the Lord...and so with every work of their hands, and what they offer there is unclean'"]: Two questions did Haggai the prophet ask them.

B. In the case of one, they answered him properly, and in the case of the other, they did not answer him properly.

C. "The skirt" is in the first remove of uncleanness [having touched some source of uncleanness].

D. "The Holy flesh" is in the second.

E. "The bread and pottage" are in the third remove.

F. "The wine, oil, and food" are in the fourth.

G. "Now," [he asked them], "Is there such a thing as a fourth remove [from the original source of uncleanness] in regard to Holy Things?"

H. They answered him, "No."

I. But they did not answer him properly, for there most certainly is a fourth remove in regard to Holy Things.

J. "Then said Haggai, If one who is unclean by contact with a dead body touches any of these, does it become unclean?"

K. [That is to say,] if the skirt of his garment should be unclean with corpse-uncleanness and touch any of these, will it impart uncleanness to them?

L. "The priests answered, 'It does become unclean.'"

M. In so saying, they answered him quite correctly.

N. [But characterizing the former answer as wrong is not necessarily so.] For R. Jeremiah, R. Hiyya in the name of R. Yohanan said, "It was in early times, in fact before [scribes] had decreed that we take account of a fourth remove [from the original source of uncleanness] in the matter of Holy Things, that he addressed his question to them. [Accordingly, they answered quite properly.]"

O. Then why does Haggai curse them [if they gave the right answer]?

P. He was in the position of someone looking for any excuse to curse his fellow.

Q. But why then did he include reference to their making the house of the Lord unclean, if in fact the law was as they said it was, that he should say to them, "And what they offer there is unclean?"

R. It was in line with that which R. Simon bar Zebedi said, "They found the skull of Arnon the Jebusite buried underneath the altar [which meant that a principal source of uncleanness contaminated all the offerings made in the Temple]."

S. [Explaining the matter differently,] R. Aha in the name of R. Abba bar Kahana: "They were expert in the law of transferring uncleanness by shifting an object, but they were not expert in the laws of transferring uncleanness by *maddaf* [which is the mode of uncleanness transferred by a *Zab, Zabah,* or menstruating person (Lev. 15), to objects used for lying or sitting (but not to food or drink) even without direct contact, located above their heads].

T. "'If one carries holy flesh in the skirt of his garment,' he asked them, 'does one unclean with corpse-uncleanness impart uncleanness to an object merely by shifting it [without direct contact with it]?'

U. "'The priests said to him, 'No.'

V. "They answered him quite correctly, for one unclean with corpse-uncleanness does not impart uncleanness to an object merely by shifting it without actual contact with it.

W. "He asked them, 'Does one who is unclean with corpse-uncleanness convey uncleanness by *maddaf* [as explained at S]?'

X. "The priests answered him, 'He does transmit uncleanness in that way.'

Y. "In this regard they did not reply to him correctly. For one unclean with corpse-uncleanness does not impart uncleanness through the mode of *maddaf* [as explained at S]."

Z. R. Tanhuma, R. Pinhas in the name of R. Levi: "It was concerning whether or not we take account of a fifth remove from the original source of uncleanness in matters of Holy Things that he asked them. And the indication is as follows:

AA. "'If one carries holy flesh in the skirt of his garment...':

BB. "'The skirt of his garment' is in the first remove.

CC. "'Holy flesh' is in the second remove.

DD. "'Bread and pottage' are in the third remove.

EE. "'Wine and oil' are in the fourth remove.

FF. "'And food' is in the fifth, [and it was in that regard that] he asked them [his question].

GG. "Now he asked them do we take account of a fifth remove in respect to Holy Things?

HH. "And the priests answer, 'No.'

II. "They answered him quite correctly, for there is no consideration of a fifth remove in Holy Things."

JJ. Then why does Haggai curse them [if they gave the right answer]?

KK. He was in the position of someone looking for any excuse to curse his fellow.

LL. But why then did he include reference to their making the house of the Lord unclean, if in fact the law was as they said it was, that he should say to them, "And what they offer there is unclean?"

MM. It was in line with that which R. Simeon bar Zebedi said, "They found the skull of Arnon the Jebusite buried underneath the altar."

**VII.**

A. It was taught: Said R. Yosé, "How do we know that that which is unclean by a source of uncleanness in the fourth remove [from the original source of uncleanness] in the case of Holy Things is invalid [= M. Hag. 3:2E-F]?

B. "And it is reasonable.

C. "Now if one who has not completed atonement rites [by bringing the required offering, e.g., a *Zab* (Lev. 15), or a woman after childbirth, Lev. 12] is not invalid in the case of heave-offering but is invalid in the case of Holy Things,

D. "that which is made unclean by a source of uncleanness in the fourth remove, which is invalid in the case of heave-offering – is it not reasonable that it should invalidate [that which touches it, in the case of Holy Things]?

E. "We have learned in Scripture (M. Sot. 5:2) that that which is made unclean by a source of uncleanness in the third remove from the original source of uncleanness invalidates, and in connection with that which is unclean in the fourth remove [we thus derive the same lesson] by an argument *a fortiori.*" (T. Hag. 3:18)

F. Objected R. Yohanan, "Food which has been touched by a Tebul Yom [unclean in the second remove, we recall] will prove the contrary.

G. "For it is invalid so far as being designated heave-offering is concerned [in line with Lev. 11:33],

H. "but it has no invalidating affect upon Holy Things [in the fourth remove. That is: Just as the Tebul Yom invalidates in the case of heave-offering, so he invalidates in the case of Holy Things. But he does not render the Holy Things unclean in such wise that the Holy Things will then go and impart uncleanness. In this case, then, the argument *a fortiori* of Yosé will not serve, as it does above, and so it is shown to be invalid.]"

I. [Providing a second attack on Yosé's reasoning,] R. Hiyya in the name of R. Yohanan, "The view of R. Yosé is in line with the theory of R. 'Aqiba, his teacher.

J. "Just as R. 'Aqiba said, '...will be unclean...' (Lev. 11:33, referring to food) means, '...will impart uncleanness...' [in the third remove, as at M. 5:2A], as a matter of the law of Torah,'

K. "so R. Yosé said, '...will be unclean...,' (Lev. 11:34) with reference to liquid, means, '...will impart uncleanness...' as a matter of the law of the Torah." [In this case why not construct the same argument *a fortiori* to prove that we take account of a fourth remove in regard to food in the status of heave-offering, and deem such food to be invalid. Now if a Tebul Yom, who is permitted to touch unconsecrated food, is invalid so far as heave-offerings is concerned, food in the third remove, which is invalid so far as unconsecrated food is concerned (in line with the position of 'Aqiba at M. 5:2A, unconsecrated food in the third remove is invalid and may not be designated heave-offering), all the more so should be deemed to invalidate food in the fourth remove for heave-offering. This then is a further argument against the reasoning of Yosé at A-E]."

L. R. Abbahu in the name of R. Yosé bar Haninah: "R. Yosé has no need for the argument *a fortiori* [to prove that that which is in the fourth remove from the original source of uncleanness in the case of Holy Things is invalid].

M. "R. Yosé is perfectly able to prove the same thing on the basis of the exegesis of the following verse of Scripture:

N. "['Flesh that touches any unclean thing shall not be eaten' (Lev. 7:19).] 'Flesh that touches' – This refers to meat in the second remove of uncleanness which touched that which is unclean in the first remove of uncleanness.

O. "'Any unclean thing' – This refers to meat in the third remove of uncleanness which touched that which was unclean in the second remove of uncleanness [as is clear in the sequence of the verse].

P. "'Shall not be eaten' – That which is made unclean at the end is not to be eaten. [That is to say, what touches this meat in the third remove, which itself is in the fourth remove, is not to be eaten. That proves the besought proposition.]"

**VIII.**

A. Up to this point we have dealt with food made clean in the air space of a clay utensil contaminated by a dead creeping thing (Lev. 11:33). [That is, 'Aqiba's prof, based on Lev. 11:33, shows that food made unclean in the contained air space of a clay utensil into which a dead creeping thing has fallen has the capacity to impart uncleanness to food which touches it.]

B. How do we know that food itself which has been made unclean by a dead creeping thing has the power to impart uncleanness to other food?

C. Now it is a matter of logic.

D. If utensils, which do not receive uncleanness when they are located in the contained air space of a clay utensil which has been rendered unclean by a dead creeping thing – lo, such utensils impart uncleanness as does a dead creeping thing so that food which touches them will be unclean,

E. food itself, which is rendered unclean by a dead creeping thing, is it not a matter of logic that it should have the capacity to impart uncleanness as does a dead creeping thing to [other] food [with which it comes into contact]? [Surely that is obvious.]

F. Up to this point we have dealt with the matter in line with the theory of R. 'Aqiba [who regards the uncleanness imparted in the third remove as a matter of the law of the Torah].

G. But as to R. Ishmael [how does he prove that there is a third remove in regard to food which has been in contact with that which has been made unclean?]

H. It is taught by R. Ishmael: "'Flesh that touches any unclean thing shall not be eaten.'

I. "[This refers to] food in the first remove, 'which touched any unclean thing.'

J. "'It shall not be eaten' is meant to encompass that which is in the second remove.

K. "And as to the third remove, how do we prove that that is taken into account?

L. "It is a matter of logical inference.

M. "Now if a Tebul Yom, who does not invalidate in the case of unconsecrated food, lo, he has the power to invalidate in the case of heave-offering [which he touches, so that said heave-offering is deemed unclean and may not be eaten,]

N. "food unclean in the second remove, which indeed is invalid in the case of unconsecrated food [as at M. Toh. 2:3ff.] – is it not logical that it should have the power to invalidate in the case of heave-offering?

O. "And as to a fourth remove in the case of Holy Things, how do we prove that proposition?

P. "Now it is a matter of logic.

Q. "If one who has not yet brought his offerings to complete the process of atonement, who is not invalid for eating heave-offering, lo, he is invalid so far as Holy Things are concerned [Lev. 12, 15, indicate that until the offerings are brought to complete the process of atonement, the woman after childbirth, the *Zab*, and *Zabah* are not permitted to eat Holy Things],

R. "that which is in the third remove from the original source of uncleanness, which indeed is invalid so far as heave-offering is concerned – is it not logical that it should have the power to invalidate in the case of Holy Things [with which it comes into contact, hence, the fourth remove]?

S. "Lo we have learned from Scripture the law governing the uncleanness of invalidity of that which is in the first remove and the second remove from the original source of uncleanness, and from a logical process we have derived the same rule for that which is in the third remove, and as to that which is in the fourth remove, we have derived the same proposition from an argument *a fortiori*.

T. "[After we have] reasoned one law from the other [deriving the rule governing the third remove in the case of heave-offering from the second remove in the case of the Tebul Yom, we derive yet another rule by means of an argument for that which is in the fourth remove, that it is invalid in the case of food in the status of Holy Things], so that all should be governed by the law,

U. "thus with the result that heave-offering is the third remove, and Holy Things in the fourth remove, should be deemed invalid."

# Part Two

# CURRENT PRACTICES IN TRANSLATING CLASSICS OF JUDAISM: THE TRANSLATION AS PARAPHRASE, PRÉCIS, AND SHOW-PIECE

# 4

# Translation as Paraphrase: Braude and Kapstein on Pesiqta and DeRab Kahana

Up to now I have not attended to a theory of translation that dismisses the text as a collection of mere suggestions and chooses to render matters in accord with the translator's (superior) sense of things. There are, specifically, translators who do not translate but who paraphrase. The distinction between translation and paraphrase makes a considerable difference.

Translation gives the text as literally as possible but in a language other than the original, paraphrase, the gist of the text, with the actual wording meant to convey an imputation of the "deeper" meaning. Translation aims at intelligibility, in the second language, of the statements of the original. Paraphrase promises more than a mere rendition of one language in the syntax and word-choices of another. It promises a judgment of meaning and sense, constituting a commentary. The difference between a translation and a paraphrase is not subjective but may be determined through a simple, objective test: can we move from the new language to the old? A translation allows a bilingual person to move from the new language to the old, a paraphrase does not. So if we can read the new language and more or less accurately recover the original text, we have a translation. If in the text given in the new language we cannot recover anything of the original, we have a paraphrase and not a translation.

The value of the one as compared to the other may be simply explained. When we translate, what purpose dictates our choices? Do we aim at a simple, literal statement, in the language and categories of one world, of the legacy of the other? Or do we impose our judgment upon questions of meaning, carrying into our language not only the words of the other, but also our imposed conception of what those words must mean to make sense to us? In my judgment the task of the present age is to translate into English, the international language of politics and culture, and also the one language spoken and read by the majority of the Jews in the world today, the classic texts of the Judaic canon. At some later time, perhaps, commentaries may take the form of paraphrases – but only when clearly labeled as commentaries. At no time is it legitimate to present a commentary and call it a translation. That constitutes a considerable misrepresentation of the facts.

The issue at hand bears profound implications for the future of Judaism and how its classic texts will reach the future near at hand. For our generation presently produces in the English language a full and complete repertoire of the classical Judaic canon; within a very short time, every single text of Judaism produced between the second and the seventh centuries – from the Mishnah through the Bavli – will be available in American English. This vast labor of translation, – as a matter of fact utterly without parallel in so brief a spell, – has been accomplished within a single generation, from the 1950s, that is, about a decade after World War II, to the present.[1] If all goes well, it will not end for the foreseeable future; for every document will demand further study, and the translations accorded will require ongoing revision. All informed scholars understand that fact; errors are easy (for *idiot-savants*) to celebrate but also easy (for serious scholars) to correct – once a basic text in American English is in hand. But ours is the generation to bring the classics of Judaism to the American language.

No other Jewish community in history brought into its native language so complete a repertoire of the classical literature of Judaism as have we; none did it so rapidly, so early in its history – for, in American English, we are scarcely more than two or three generations old, with Yiddish speaking grandparents or great-grandparents, and, commonly, parents who did not go to college. We are by no means the first great Jewish community to live its Judaism in its own language; the

[1]The Soncino Bavli and Midrash-Rabbah translations were done prior to World War II, but they seem to me to mark the true beginning of the rendition into English of the classics of Judaism. I do not know the history of the translation of those same classics into German. The pages of this book – Chapter Two, for instance – should suggest, however, that I see a break between the Soncino work and that begun by me in the early 1970s. The present chapter as well as my discussion of Goldin in the next chapter and Hammer in later on will explain why I found no important guidance, as to a theory of translation, in anyone prior to myself or in contemporaries either.

Arabic-speaking world of Jewry did;[2] the Yiddish-speaking world of Eastern Europe did, and so did the German Jewish community which, for nearly a century and a half, from ca. 1800 to ca. 1940, defined Jewish scholarship.[3] But we are distinguished, I believe, by the rapidity and completeness with which we have made our own, in our own language

---

[2]The history of its translation of the Judaic classics into Arabic is not known to me. I do not have the impression that within a hundred years of the arrival of the Arabic language within the realm of Judaic discourse, the classics were all in Arabic, even though some of the greatest intellectual figures in Judaism in that context wrote their most important work in Arabic.

[3]We do not know what might have been and therefore cannot say whether or not, had the German scholarship in Judaism not been wiped out in World War II, it would have retained the influence it had in its heyday. But the post-World War II history of German scholarship in the humanities and social sciences has proved so dismal that I doubt that the German Jewish school could have retained the interest of world scholarship. That is virtually certain, since their heirs and continuators in the State of Israel have been reduced to collecting variant readings and producing compilations of sources; their "history" is worse than merely uncritical and gullible; it is dull and witless; they do not work on Judaism as a religion at all; and even in the fields of Judaic learning that they claim to do better than anyone else, publishing critical texts for instance, they prove unproductive. So my sense is that the humanities in the German tradition have pretty much run their course, and if the German Jewish school had survived in Germany, we should not find much guidance and inspiration in their ideas and methods. The contrast with the French humanities in this context is stunning. There a vast and influential world of thought and learning flourishes; but none of this is mediated into Judaic studies, so far as I can see. At least, we overseas are able to find in the writings (such as they are) of specialists on the study of the Jews and Judaism in France none of that incisive and fundamental insight that has made French humanistic learning (philosophy, for example) the standard and the model for the entire world of letters. Judaic studies in the French language prove as narrow, parochial, and ethnically self-celebratory as the work done in German and, for the study of late antiquity, in Israeli Hebrew as well. I can understand why specialists in late antique Judaism in the State of Israel, with their deadening inheritance from the German humanities in the period between World War I and World War II, have so little to say to anybody. But I cannot make sense of an entire community of Judaic Studies, in the French language, in which we perceive so little impact from the cultural context, which is the vivid and engaging world of learning of France today. Judaic studies in the Italian language and also in Spanish, by contrast, appear, for late antiquity, fresh and interesting, and I am hopeful that we shall learn much from colleagues in Italy, Spain, and even in Latin America in due course. Indeed, I regard the near accident that I decided to study Portuguese, which has given me access to Spanish, as a splendid serendipity in my scholarly pilgrimage.

and therefore our distinctive intellectual categories, nearly the whole of the received holy writings of the Judaism of talmudic times – the Targumim, the Talmuds, the midrashim, and the rest: all of it is now in American English, or soon will be. We have done it, in a single generation. Now, as I shall explain, we begin the work of doing it all over again, a work that will continue so long as American Jewry flourishes in the life of the intellect.

For how we render a document from its original language to ours dictates how we shall adapt the document and its meanings for our own purposes. And that process goes on without limit. It follows that the purpose and character of these translations will govern the way in which the classical writings of Judaism reach Jewry for the next hundred years. Since the majority of world Jewry lives in the English language, the work presently under way will make a deep impact upon the shape of Judaism, in all its versions and forms, for the coming century – and perhaps long afterward as well.

In my view a translation should serve as a clear, literal rendition in the one language of what is written in the other: rendition, not paraphrase, not interpretation, not commentary, not "great literature." Translation should moreover facilitate ready reference to every line of the document, so that analytical studies in American English can be undertaken by specialists in other subjects; the texts must not only be made available, they also should be opened up and unlocked for general examination and inquiry. I have just completed two translations of works that, in general, already are familiar to the American reader. Both of them constitute sustained criticism of prior translations of the same documents. The one is *The Fathers According to Rabbi Nathan, An Analytical Translation and Explanation* (Atlanta, 1986: Scholars Press). The other, *Pesiqta deRab Kahana, An Analytical Translation and Explanation* (Atlanta, 1986: Scholars Press) I-III, is the first complete and systematic translation of the authoritative and critical Pesiqta deRab Kahana, that is, the one published by Bernard Mandelbaum, *Pesikta de Rab Kahana. According to An Oxford Manuscript. With Variants from All Known Manuscripts and Genizoth Fragments and Parallel Passages. With Commentary and Introduction* (New York, 1962: The Jewish Theological Seminary of America) I-II. I owe an explanation of why I found it necessary to translate texts that already exist in English, since, in the nature of things, my work testifies to a rejection of aspects of the translation of prior students of the same documents (if a strong affirmation of other aspects of those translations).

Let me begin[4] with a clear statement of how I shall know I have succeeded in my goals. I reiterate the text I stated above. A successful translation leads the reader to a clear picture of the original language of the text. The test of my success in both cases will derive from the possibility of returning to, or envisioning, the Hebrew from the English. My translation, while meant to make sense in English, should pass that test. I mean further to make possible a systematic description of, and introduction to, the document, and the comparison of the document to others of its genus and species within the canon of the Judaism of the Dual Torah, the classification of the document within its larger genus. Since there are two versions in English of both documents, let me explain why I found it necessary to make my new ones, which I believe are more accurate as translations and more serviceable for study and analysis than those now available.

Pesikta deRab Kahana illustrates the choices before us as translators. As I shall explain, it also shows us precisely how not to translate, though it also provides us with a first rate commentary – and précis of existing commentaries, not always given full credit for their contributions – in the guise of a translation. The prior English rendition, William G. (Gershon Zev) Braude and Israel J. Kapstein, *Pesikta de-Rab Kahana. R. Kahana's Compilation of Discourses for Sabbaths and Festal Days* (Philadelphia, 1975: Jewish Publication Society of America) simply is no translation at all.[5] That is why mine is in fact the first translation into English of the Hebrew text. There are three problems with the Braude and Kapstein[6] rendition, which, I

---

[4]Goldin is presently treated in a separate chapter. Originally I dealt with both together.

[5]Braude's earlier translations, *Midrash on Psalms* for example, were much more loyal to the Hebrew text. His later work was also his worst, and I do not know why he changed his mind about how he thought translation should be carried on. The earlier work was much more disciplined, the later, rather self-indulgent. My guess is that the disciplines of scholarship could not overcome the temptations of the pulpit; Braude's representation of Midrash-passages in sermons that I heard were enchanting and conveyed, I thought, an authentic sense of what might have been. But in translation we really want to present not what might have been but what was, and here Braude seems to me to have wandered from his original program.

[6]Kapstein, an English professor at Brown University, of course contributed to the English but not to the Hebrew, which he did not know as a scholar. Perhaps it was his influence that so drastically distorted the representation of the Hebrew. But my sense is that Braude did things as he wanted them to be done, so we cannot blame Kapstein for more than his fair share of the mess that resulted.

maintain, is a commentary in the form of a paraphrase, but not a translation in any serious sense.

First, they have not *translated* the text that is before us. Let me explain. When I turned to the study of Pesiqta deRab Kahana for my larger study of the formation of Judaism, I found it useless because it is far too much of a paraphrase, harmonizing and unifying what are really distinct and unrelated passages, solving textual problems by imputing verbiage with no counterpart in the Hebrew, and other exercises in circumlocution, to permit systematic analytical description and study of the document. That fact necessitated my rereading and fresh translation of the original Hebrew. That earlier version, while rich in stylistic originality and other merits of attractive rendition of the sense or the gist of the Hebrew, does not really translate the actual Hebrew text from one language into the other; proof is that reversing the process, moving out of English into Hebrew, leads us far away from the actual Hebrew text, which, out of the English, we can scarcely imagine. What they have done is not a translation but a paraphrastic rendition, more of a literary and rabbinical than an academic and scholarly translation. They do not address an academic audience but a lay and literary one. So we cannot criticize them for not accomplishing what they to begin with did not set out to do.

Not only is Braude and Kapstein's rendering not a translation, but there is a second, still more compelling consideration to require a translation of the document. They have not translated the best critical *text* of our document. In fact it is difficult to know precisely what version or text, at any given point, they do claim to translate. The Hebrew text on which Braude's and Kapstein's translation is based *appears* to be eclectic,[7] therefore is not readily available to scholars in general, rather than systematic and commonly accessible. I say *appears*, because they do not explicitly state that it is Bernard Mandelbaum's. Alas, their English is commonly so loosely related to the Hebrew that we cannot guess what other text, besides Mandelbaum's, they might have had in hand.[8] In their English

[7] I say "appears to be," because their rendition is so loosely tied to the Hebrew that I cannot reconstruct the Hebrew out of the English.

[8] But Mandelbaum demonstrated in private correspondence, which I have seen, that Braude and Kapstein were translating from his critical text and making use of his notes (some of them credited, in fact, to Saul Lieberman). A very rancorous correspondence, complete with threats of law-suits, marred the reception of Braude's and Kapstein's book, and Mandelbaum never got from them the credit that they owed him. The episode did no credit to Braude. This kind of shabby treatment of colleagues is not uncommon, and it should be

translation of the work, Braude and Kapstein, the translators do not indicate what text is translated, and, while referring to Mandelbaum's edition as "an admirable achievement," "superior to Buber's," "more accurately and more amply edited," Braude and Kapstein do not allege that they have translated Mandelbaum's text, beginning, middle, and end. I have done just that, so that readers who wish to compare my translation to the original Hebrew can do so – and improve on my rendering. Because of the paraphrastic approach to translation chosen by the earlier translators, the differences between Mandelbaum's text of Pesiqta deRab Kahana and the (apparently) eclectic text developed by Braude and Kapstein will not be easy to follow up. But where the differences are substantive and considerable, they will be readily apparent.

Let me give a concrete example of what I believe is simple "overinterpretation," or improving upon the Hebrew and imputing to it a sense – continuity, harmony, cogency – that the Hebrew does not contain. It derives from the linkage of two discourses I believe should stand independent of one another.

II:VI

1. A. R. Yudan opened discourse by citing the following verse of Scripture: *A good man's tongue is pure silver, the heart of the wicked is trash. [The lips of a good man teach many, but fools perish for want of sense]* (Prov. 10:20):

B. "*A good man's tongue is pure silver* speaks of Jedo the prophet (2 Chr. 9:29).

C. "...*the heart of the wicked is trash* refers to Jeroboam (1 Kgs. 12:28-29)."

D. *As Jeroboam stood by the altar to burn the sacrifice, a man of God from Judah, moved by the word of the Lord, appeared at Bethel. He inveighed against the altar in the Lord's name, crying out, "O altar, altar! [This is the word of the Lord: 'Listen! A child shall be born to the house of David, named Josiah. He will sacrifice upon you the priests of the hill-shrines who make offerings upon you, and he will make human bones upon you.'" He gave a sign the same day: 'This is the sign which the Lord has ordained: This altar will be rent in pieces and the ashes upon it will be spilt.' When King Jeroboam heard the sentence which the man of God pronounced against the altar at Bethel, he pointed to him from the altar and said, 'Seize that man!' Immediately the hand which*

---

remembered. I believe that by translating Mandelbaum's text and by submitting my translation for his line by line correction, I did represent Pesiqta deRab Kahana precisely as Mandelbaum thought it should be set forth.

*he had pointed at him became paralyzed, so that he could not draw it back. The altar too was rent in pieces and the ashes were spilt, in fulfilment of the sign that the man of God had given at the Lord's command]* (1 Kgs. 13:1-5).

E. Why does it say, *altar, altar,* two times?

F. Said R. Abba bar Kahana, "One alludes to the altar in Beth El, the other to the altar in Dan."

G. And what was the prophet's proclamation? *"O altar, altar! This is the word of the Lord: 'Listen! A child shall be born to the house of David, named Josiah. He will sacrifice upon you the priests of the hill-shrines who make offerings upon you, and he will make human bones upon you.'"*

H. "The bones *of Jeroboam* will be burned on you" is not what is stated, but rather, *he will make human bones upon you.*

I. This teaches that he paid all due respect to the monarchy.

J. It is written, *When King Jeroboam heard the sentence which the man of God pronounced against the altar at Bethel, he pointed to him from the altar and said, 'Seize that man!'*

K. R. Huna in the name of R. Idi: "The Omnipresent had more concern for the honor owing to the righteous man than to the honor owing to himself. For when he [the king] was standing and offering a sacrifice to idolatry, his hand did not dry up. But when he put his hand against that righteous man [the prophet], then his hand dried up.

L. "So it is written: *'Immediately the hand which he had pointed at him became paralyzed, so that he could not draw it back.'*"

M. *The king appealed to the man of God to pacify the Lord your God' and pray for him that his hand might be restored. [The man of God did as he asked; his hand was restored and became as it had been before. Then the king said to the man of God, 'Come home and take refreshment at my table and let me give you a present.' But the man of God answered, 'If you were to give me half your house, I would not enter it with you; I will eat and drink nothing in this place, for the Lord's command to me was to eat and drink nothing and not to go back by the way I came.' So he went back another way; he did not return by the road he had taken to Bethel]* (1 Kgs. 13:6-10).

N. Two Amoras: one said, "The meaning of the reference to *the Lord your God* is, *your God,* not mine."

O. The other said, "By what sort of brazenness could he have called him, 'my God,' while he was standing and offering to an idol? Could he then have called him 'my God'?"

P. Nonetheless: *The man of God did as he asked; his hand was restored and became as it had been before.*

Q. What is the meaning of the statement, *as it had been before?*

R. R. Berekhiah, R. Judah b. R. Simon in the name of R. Joshua b. Levi: "'Even though you beat a fool in the mortar of a craftsman, you will make nothing of him.' Just as, in the beginning, he would stand and make offerings to idolatry, so even afterward he would stand and make offerings to an idol."

2. A. Another interpretation of *A good man's tongue is pure silver* refers to the Holy One, blessed be he, who chose the tongue of Moses and said, *When you raise up the head of the children of Israel (Ex. 30:12).*

The intersecting verse reverts to the base verse only at No. 2, while the far more fully articulated exposition, No. 1, reads the intersecting verse in the light of an entirely unrelated matter. The reader will want to know that, when citing biblical verses, I quote far more than is given in the manuscripts; these allude through a few words to a larger verse, and the important clause of the verse may not always appear in the text at hand.

The problem of the translator, as Braude and Kapstein see things, is to link No. 1 to No. 2, so establishing what is in their mind a unitary *and also intelligible* text. Accordingly, Braude and Kapstein translate the operative language of No. 2 as follows:

> This is to say that the Holy One [not at all concerned with the respect due to Him], saw to it that Moses chose words [as precious as choice silver and as dazzling in the unexpected favor they showed to Israel]: When Thou liftest the head tax from the children of Israel, [Thou also liftest their heads].

Let me state what they have done wrong with appropriate emphasis:

*What they have attempted is to link the two* distinct *compositions, introducing the theme of the former into the latter, and, further, they have imputed a meaning to No. 2 which I do not see in the text.*

My sense is that they err by making more sense of the materials before us than the naked eye discerns. This is a good example of what I maintain is simply a translation that makes more sense than and so improves upon the original Hebrew.

My third reason to reject their work as translation is simply stated. I have the strong sense that the document is not so accessible as they render it.[9] They find more sense in the Hebrew than I think can be

[9]That often is also my most serious criticism of my own translations, particularly in the Talmud of the Land of Israel. I had two concerns. First, I hoped (and thought) that I rendered accurately not only the words but, more important, the sense and meaning of the text. Second, I did not wish to represent as

demonstrated to be present. So through paraphrase and imaginative renderings, they impute clarity, ubiquitous continuity, and even harmony, that the Hebrew does not provide, solve problems that the Hebrew does not permit to be solved, and, in all, give us rather more than, in the Hebrew, meets the eye. I prefer to give what I see and to allow the reader in on the secret that not every word is equally clear, not every statement equally accessible as to sense and meaning, in the text as we presently have it.

My basic approach to translation is entirely different from theirs, which, as I said, accounts for the necessity to retranslate the work in its entirety. The difference is more than a matter of taste or style in how one should translate.[10] It is whether one is translating at all when the translator imputes to the text at hand a vast range of meanings and conceptions contributed only by the later commentaries, or by the translator serving as commentator. Obviously, every translation is also a commentary. But there seem to me limits to the sort of commentary one provides in the guise of a translation, and because Braude and Kapstein find no guidance in the restraints of the original language, they have given us something other than a translation. It is a

---

comprehensible what in fact is not comprehensible. My translation was criticized for errors in the rendition of some words and phrases, and these criticisms are helpful and important. But no reviewer has yet made the case that I simply did not understand the document before me, and that would have been a weighty criticism indeed. None has claimed that I made sense out of nonsense, and that too would have been a serious criticism. So, overall, the critical reception has proven merely interesting, if in the balance rather light-weight, but perceptive and important in no negative aspect. And the positive reviews have vastly outweighed the negative ones in volume and in substance.

[10]But I do not agree with Braude and Kapstein, or with Goldin, that the best mode of translation is to pretend to be producing literature. My goal has been to render texts into fluent and colloquial American English while remaining as close to the original as I can. I want to present the ancient rabbis as they would have spoken simple and accessible American English. They did not leave us literature, they left us writings meant for a different purpose altogether than that of literature. Specifically, these are religious writings written by religious men for the purpose of making a holy society and sacred community of Israel, and to them matters of exquisite expression (for example) made a difference only when through saying things in one way rather than some other they could register a profound religious insight or a compelling religious attitude. To pretend that they were belle-lettristic authors is to misrepresent them, and the studied elegance of Braude's and Kapstein's representations and also of Goldin's leads us away, and not toward, the heart and soul of these writings. A fundamental secularity characterizes the transformation of religious documents into mere literature.

commentary in the form of a paraphrase, something new and different if, for purposes of academic study, not terribly useful. Let me now show in detail the contrast between their approach and mine.

**Braude and Kapstein, p. 31**

Pisqa II:VII

> In the phrase *the head* (Exod. 30:12), so said R. Jose bar Hanina, it is intimated that Moses would bring back into Israel's midst the head – that is, the oldest one – of the Tribe Fathers. Who was that? Reuben, of course, of whom at the end of Moses' life, Moses was to say, *Let Reuben live:* [let his sin in lying with Bilhah be remembered no more] *and let his people be reckoned in the numbering [of Israel]* (Deut. 33:6).

At *[of Israel]* they add the following note: See Rashi on Deut. 33:6, and Gen. 35:22.

My translation of the same passage is as follows:

2. A. *[When you raise up] the head [of the children of Israel] [and take a census]* (Ex. 30:12).
   B. Said R. Yosé bar Haninah, "This statement served to provide an indication that [Moses] was going to draw near [restoring primacy to] the first of the tribes, and who is that? It is Reuben:
   C. "*Let Reuben live* (Deut. 33:6)."

The first difference is in my insistence on giving, in English, only what is in the Hebrew.

The second, as I said, is that I follow a single, consistent text. Specifically, I believe that Mandelbaum's position that certain materials contained in only a single manuscript do not form part of Pesiqta deRab Kahana should be taken into account in presenting an English version of the same; Braude and Kapstein differ, and so translate sizable selections of materials that, from a critical viewpoint, enjoy only a dubious claim to a place in our document.

The third point of difference is in the paraphrastic harmonization of discrete pericopae, a constant feature of Braude's and Kapstein's translation to which I have already alluded. The following rendition seems to me not a translation at all.

**Braude and Kapstein, p. 18**

Pisqa I:VIII

> At the same time Moses was distraught but for a different reason. He said: The Holy Spirit must have departed from me, and having come to rest upon the princes, [inspired them to bring the wagons and the

oxen]. Whereupon the Holy One said: "Moses, if I had wanted the princes to bring their offerings, I would have asked you to tell them so. But what I now tell you is *Purchase; it is of them* (Num. 7:5): The idea of offerings came from the 'them' [referred to elsewhere in Scripture, and not from the princes]." Who, then, are meant by "them"? The Tribe of Issachar who gave the idea to the princes, the Tribe of whom Scripture says, *And of the children of Issachar came men who had understanding of the times* (1 Chron. 12:33). What is meant by *the times*? The right times for doing what should be done, according to R. Tanhuma; intercalary days and months, according to R. Jose bar Kasri. Concerning the tribe of Issachar, Chronicles goes on: *the heads of them were two hundred (ibid.)*, implies that their brethren in Israel were to conduct themselves in keeping with the practical advice given them by Issachar. It was the Tribe of Issachar, then, [and not the holy spirit] which said to the princes: "This Tent of Meeting that you see being made--how is it to move about? Is it to fly in the air? Make wagons for it and carry its parts therein."

My translation is as follows:

I:VIII

4. A. *And the Lord spoke to Moses and said, ["Accept these from them: they shall be used for the service of the tent of the presence"]* (Num. 7:5).
   B. What is the meaning of the word, *and said*?
   C. R. Hoshaia taught, "The Holy One, blessed be he, said to Moses, 'Go and say to Israel words of praise and consolation.'
   D. "Moses was afraid, saying, 'But is it not possible that the holy spirit has abandoned me and come to rest on the chiefs?'
   E. "The Holy One said to him, 'Moses, Had I wanted them to bring their offering, I should have said to you to 'say to them,' [so instructing them to do so], but *Take – it is from them [at their own volition, not by my inspiration]* (Num. 7:5) is language that bears the meaning, they did it on their own volition [and have not received the holy spirit].'"

5. A. And who gave them the good ideas [of making the gift]?
   B. It was the tribe of Simeon who gave them the good idea, in line with this verse: *And of the children of Issachar came men who had understanding of the times* (1 Chr. 12:33).
   C. What is the sense of *the times*?
   D. R. Tanhuma said, "The ripe hour [*kairos*]."
   E. R. Yosé bar Qisri said, "Intercalating the calendar."
   F. *They had two hundred heads* (1 Chr. 12:33):
   G. This refers to the two hundred heads of sanhedrins that were produced by the tribe of Issachar.
   H. *And all of their brethren were subject to their orders* (1 Chr. 12:33):
   I. This teaches that the law would accord with their rulings.

J. They said to the community, "Is this tent of meeting which you are making going to fly in the air? Make wagons for it, which will bear it."

The differences are blatant. Readers who go to the Hebrew text will recognize the words I have translated, I believe with exact, meticulous concern for detail. They will be hard put to find in the Hebrew the words that, in Braude's and Kapstein's rendition, are represented in the English. I see many merits in the interpretative rendition of Braude and Kapstein; I believe their sense of the passage at hand has much to recommend it; it certainly joins what to me are discrete items. In the passage at hand, I have no doubt that their basic theory of the sense and meaning is sound. But while I maintain that Braude and Kapstein have given us a first-rate paraphrase, I find it self-evident that theirs is not a translation at all. And, as I have said, I believe a translation should be just that: no less, no more.

Let me give one further example by showing the effect upon their translation of their insistence that we have a seamless and unitary text, not a composite of diverse materials joined together, as seems to me blatantly obvious, by the ultimate compositors. For this purpose I give my translation alone, with reference to how Braude and Kapstein treat the matter.

I:II.

1. A. *King Solomon made a pavilion for himself* (Song 3:9) [The New English Bible: *The palanquin which King Solomon had made for himself was of wood from Lebanon. Its poles he made of silver, its head-rest of gold; its seat was of purple stuff, and its lining was of leather*]:

B. *Pavilion* refers to the tent of meeting.

C. *King Solomon made a...for himself:* he is the king to whom peace [*shalom/shelomoh*] belongs.

2. A. Said R. Judah bar Ilai, "[The matter may be compared to the case of] a king who had a little girl. Before she grew up and reached puberty, he would see her in the market place and chat with her, or in alleyways and chat with her. But when she grew up and reached puberty, he said, 'It is not fitting for the dignity of my daughter that I should talk with her in public. Make a pavilion for her, so that I may chat with her in the pavilion.'

B. "So, to begin with: *When Israel was a child in Egypt, then in my love of him, I used to cry out* ((Hos. 11:1). In Egypt they saw me: *And I passed through the land of Israel* (Ex. 12:12). At the sea they saw me: *And Israel saw the great hand* (Ex. 14:31). At Sinai they saw me: *Face to face the Lord spoke with you* (Deut. 5:4).

C. "But when they received the Torah, they became a fully grown nation for me. So he said, 'It is not appropriate to the dignity of my children that I should speak with them in public. But make me a tabernacle, and I shall speak from the midst of the tabernacle.'

D. "That is in line with this verse: *And when Moses entered the tent of the presence to speak with God, he heard the voice speaking from above the cover over the ark of the tokens from between the two cherubim: the voice spoke to him* (Num. 7:89)."

Seen by itself, No. 1 has no bearing upon the larger context, but it does provide a good exegesis of Song 3:9 in terms of the theme at hand, the tabernacle. The point of No. 2 is that the purpose of the tabernacle was to make possible appropriate communication between a mature Israel and God. Then the two items are simply distinct workings of the theme of the tabernacle, one appealing to Song 3:9, the other, Num. 7:89.

But – not surprisingly – Braude and Kapstein so translate as to *link* the two:

> King Solomon made Himself: that is, the King of the universe needing a means of private communication [with Israel] made it for himself. In explanation of the verse, R. Judah bar Ilai told the parable, etc.

The footnotes justify *made Himself*, referring to God, and *communicate* out of the letters of the word translated as peace, by appeal to allegedly pertinent parallels. I find myself puzzled by the mode of argument, all the more so, the result, since it seems to me little more than free association. Erudite and inventive but uncontrolled and far-fetched, exercises of this sort will not detain us. So much for what is at stake in the difference between translation and paraphrase. But, in the balance, we have to regard Braude and Kapstein as essentially light-weights. We turn now to a weightier translator and his failure.

# 5

# Translation to Whom it May Concern: Goldin on Avot Derabbi Nathan

In the case of *The Fathers According to Rabbi Nathan*, my fresh translation was required for several important reasons. On the strength of Goldin's presentation of the document, no further analytical studies were possible, and his notes were jejune and unhelpful. But the most important was that Goldin had no particular purpose or audience in mind; hence he translated merely "to whom it may concern." His translation shows the importance of allowing a particular audience and purpose to guide the translator's work – as in point of fact such a well-considered intention inevitably guides all useful translations. That is not to suggest Goldin's translation was useless. But his *The Fathers According to Rabbi Nathan* (New Haven, 1955: Yale University Press), despite its literary and philological merits, which are not negligible, lacks any sort of reference system.

That means Goldin did not consider it likely that anyone would use his text for any purpose other than reference. He did not make it possible for analytical work of any kind to proceed, for we have no way of identifying and then signifying the units of thought that comprise paragraphs, the paragraphs that comprise complete expositions or compositions, and so on upward. On that basis, I claim, Goldin had no particular audience in mind. Goldin's translation gives us long columns of words differentiated only by paragraphs, with no numbering system to allow even allusion to a given paragraph. Thus we are left with The Fathers According to Rabbi Nathan, Chapter Four (Goldin p. 19), as our sole reference system, and that will permit no analytical exercises whatsoever. My sense is that Goldin did not conceive that such exercises would be possible; his occasional guesses on why one passage is joined to another are unsystematic and episodic.

I simply do not understand why when Goldin published his translation, he did not think it important to make possible ready reference to the units of thought of which his document was made. But he is not to be blamed in particular. Before my translations of rabbinic documents, I know of no translator[1] who provided a reference system beyond the received one of the printed texts in the Hebrew. The system in use for centuries for the Bible surely is adequate for the purpose. Further, in his rather perfunctory introduction, Goldin ignores analytical questions, concentrating, as he chose to do, on a different set altogether.

Since the one question I wish to answer through an acute and detailed demonstration of the facts is the redactional principle by which the compilers or authorship of the document made its selections and found its document cogent,[2] I found I had to reread everything from the beginning. Goldin's footnotes – there is no commentary at all – provide parallel references, with a few more ambitious exercises, nearly entirely made up of philological *apercus*. My analytical commentary systematically accounts for the work of compilation: what made the framers put things together as they did, how did they know what fit together, and what principle of conglomeration and

[1] Or even editor of a critical text! Theodor-Albeck do not do so for Genesis Rabbah, and I did not find Margulies' system for Leviticus Rabbah adequate. Saul Lieberman's system for the Tosefta demands a double system – chapter and paragraph in Zuckermandel's edition, on the one side, but also line and page in Lieberman's edition, on the other. Thus we have to give Tos. R.H. 1:1/Lieberman, p. 13, l.4 (by way of a fabricated example). And that "system" still does not differentiate the components, e.g., one line is the end of one unit of thought, the next the beginning of another. So the reference systems that do function do not allow us to identify any analytically consequential facts, even whether a sentence appears at the beginning, middle, or end of a passage. That explains why I find the so-called "critical-texts" not very helpful for critical study. The text-editors who do give us page and line references (which from an analytical viewpoint do not identify what we are looking at in context and therefore do not mean much) did better than any translators known to me, e.g., William G. Braude's translations of midrash-collections, and the Soncino translations of the Talmud of Babylonia and of the midrash-materials collected under the name Midrash Rabbah. I find all of this rather amateurish.

[2] I expand on this point in Chapter Ten. I do maintain that we can translate in such a way as to give access, in English, to both the formal and the logical characteristics of a piece of writing, and in Chapter Ten I shall make that point stick.

composition explains what we have in hand: *why this, not that.* I therefore found it necessary to retranslate the entire text because I have had my own set of goals, which required a fresh rendering of the text into English.

Goldin moreover failed in his introduction and footnotes to address to the text, in any way I can discern, a broad range of analytical questions important to any user of a translation, e.g., concerning redaction, formulation, composition, purpose, and on and on. His introduction to the history and character of the text is utterly uncritical.[3] But the literary analysis is not much more adequate to the task. As I said, he gives us long columns of words differentiated only by paragraphs, translated into the idiom he selected as appropriate, but otherwise, essentially allowed to speak for themselves to whom it may concern. His commentary – and every translation is a commentary – extends only to the meanings of words and phrases. One can only express thanks to him for the important work that he did accomplish, which is a thorough and reliable exegesis of the document, word for word and phrase for phrase, in the English language. Let me state my judgment once more with emphasis:

*In Goldin's introduction, and therefore also in his representation of the document in his translation, he asked no important questions beyond the ones concerning philology, so he presents what, in translation, is the counterpart to that scholarship of show and tell, of hunting, gathering, and arranging, that, in general, in his generation and in ours, defined the scholarly program of the ethnic approach to "Jewish studies."*

True, Goldin does translate, unlike Braude and Kapstein, who do not translate. And his translation has far more integrity and loyalty to the Hebrew than do the translators of Pesqa deRab Kahana. In providing a second translation, I in no way suggest that I found material fault with Goldin's, except in his failure to provide a reference system, on the one side, and his failure to make possible an analytical inquiry into the document, on the other. I certainly did benefit from Goldin's translation, as future commentator-translators of the document will benefit from mine as they render it obsolete just as I have made his obsolete. True, for reasons spelled out in the preceding chapter, his

---

[3]I deal with Hammer's introduction in Chapter Nine and in the Appendix; I could as well have dealt with Goldin's, for Hammer is within the same school and treats the same propositions as self-evident. One of them, I am sorry to notice, is not to quote or cite or read or learn from scholars outside of the school to which he adheres. He has paid a heavy price in learning, though perhaps from his perspective, the politics is its own reward.

preference for translating into Elizabethan English is not shared by me, and I found the translation often stilted and jejune. But I would not have undertaken to retranslate a rabbinic document already in English merely because I prefer to translate, so interpret, in the most contemporary and earthy language I can find the sages of ancient Judaism in English. I do not grasp Goldin's reasoning in this regard; it seems to me to have limited merit from a literary viewpoint, none from an academic one. But who is to debate matters of taste? In any event debate with Goldin is hardly possible, since he cites very few scholars and deliberately ignores most of the work done since 1960 in the field to which he claims to contribute. So perhaps the absence of a clearly identified audience is because Goldin never wanted to communicate beyond the limits of a very small circle of devotees. But then why translate at all?

In the balance, Goldin's work on words and phrases is exemplary and enduring. Like all future scholars of this text, I made constant reference to it, always with thanks for what he accomplished. But the translation left much work to be undertaken because, on the basis of what Goldin did provide, one could not undertake a single sustained analytical inquiry. What he did not propose to do, he also did not make possible for others to undertake. That is what renders his translation hopeless except in the one way in which, to begin with, Goldin defined his task: an elegant and interesting rendition of words and phrases. This he did, and we all enjoy the result as we do the rest of the work for ourselves.

Having explained what Goldin did wrong in failing to provide a reference system and what that failure represents, let me now explain in general terms[4] my reference system, used in both translations (as well as in my translations of the Mishnah, five tractates of the Bavli, twenty-nine tractates of the Yerushalmi, five divisions of the Tosefta, the whole of Genesis Rabbah, the whole of Leviticus Rabbah, Sifra, Sifré to Numbers, Pesiqta deRab Kahana, The Fathers According to Rabbi Nathan, and various other canonical documents, whole or in parts). The simple system aims at allowing immediate reference to any sentence (completed whole unit of thought) or still larger composite.

To accomplish this goal I have marked each whole unit of thought, then each completed and cogent statement ("paragraph" or sizable composition), and upward to each chapter. For the chapters I of course follow Schechter's division of ARNA and Mandelbaum's for PRK. I likewise follow their gross paragraphing. Both of these matters are

[4]I have already spelled out its application to Lamentations Rabbah. It serves equally everywhere, so far as I can see.

signified with Roman numerals, thus **I:I** refers to Chapter One, the first indented body of materials, **I:II**, Chapter One, the second indented body, and so on. Within each such indented body of materials are subdivisions, each of them a fully autonomous and complete thought. These I mark with an Arabic numeral. Then subdivisions of these complete thoughts – those smallest whole units of thought to which I referred – are marked with a letter, thus in all: **I:I.1.A** and so on. This permits us to refer to each sentence, both by itself and in the larger paragraph and still larger composite in which it is found. We can further characterize and identify the composites and compare them with one another. None of this is possible with Goldin's translation or Braude's and Kapstein's paraphrase.

More than ever, I am persuaded that, in the rabbinic canon, we have the notes for great music – but *not* the music. That we, as the musicians of the day, have not to recreate but to create as if out of nothing but our imagination, disciplined by learning and critical acumen. For no quartet, with its silences and its rhythms and its inner logic, exists on the printed page. It comes to life as music only in the enchanted moment of performance. There alone the music lives. And the theology of Judaism, which endures in *The Fathers According to Rabbi Nathan* and in *Pesiqta de Rab Kahana*, also demands realization. At stake in this odd component of the rabbinic canon is more than a set of literary-critical problems. We have the printed notes, but we have to train ourselves to hear the music. To begin with, that means paying attention to the notes that preserve it.

# 6

## Translation as Précis: Levertoff on Sifré to Numbers

All initial efforts at the representation, in another language, of the original must be deemed preliminary. For to translate from language to language is to mediate from one system of expression and thought to another, and that work, parlous and uncertain even when accomplished with documents of a contemporary and nearby origin, such as from French or German to English, presents special problems when under study are writings of a long-distant age and utterly alien venue. When, moreover, a long tradition of what the texts are supposed to say and mean, of what is important in and about the texts, intervenes to impose its anachronistic considerations on the original – therefore also on the generation of mediation – problems turn from chronic to acute. No wonder that we Americans recognize the challenges at hand and state at the outset our conception of our work. It is to begin, not to end, that process of hermeneutics and interpretation represented by translation of what we take to be the heritage of humanity in its encounter with Scripture.

But a preliminary translation need not misrepresent the very character and contents of the text. But, claiming to translate Sifré to Numbers, Paul P. Levertoff, *Midrash Sifre on Numbers. Selections from Early Rabbinic Scriptural Interpretations.* With an Introduction by G. H. Box (London, 1916) really just gives us a précis of the document. He did the work in such a way as not merely to abridge the Hebrew but to misrepresent its contents by skipping passages without saying so. So even the passages that are translated are not completely represented in English. Not only so, but Levertoff skipped the hard parts. Furthermore, like other translators of that pioneering generation, Levertoff tended to paraphrase, rather than aiming at a complete and literal rendition of the Hebrew. Thus, for the opening paragraph of the document:

**Levertoff:**

1

> *"Command the children of Israel that they put out of the camp every leper...that they defile not their camps in the midst whereof I dwell."*
>
> What manner of love has God bestowed upon Israel that even when they are defiled the Shekina rests upon them; cf. also Lev. xvi, 16: "Who dwelt with them in the midst of their impurity"; also Lev. xv, 31; Num. xxxv, 34.

**Neusner:**

I:XI.1

A. "[You shall put out both male and female, putting them outside the camp, that they may not defile their camp,] in the midst of which I dwell. [And the people of Israel did so and drove them outside the camp, as the Lord said to Moses, so the people of Israel did]" (Gen. 5:3-4).

B. So beloved is Israel that even though they may become unclean, the Presence of God remains among them.

C. And so Scripture states, "...who dwells with them in the midst of their uncleanness" (Lev. 16:16).

D. And further: "...by making my sanctuary unclean, which [nonetheless] is in their midst " (Lev. 15:31).

E. And it further says: "...that they may not defile their camp, in the midst of which I dwell" (Num. 5:3-4).

F. And it further says, "You shall not defile the land in which you live, in the midst of which I dwell, for I the Lord dwell in the midst of the people of Israel" (Num. 35:34).

Clearly, it would appear that Levertoff has skipped a fair amount of the text he claims to present. That failure on his part characterizes his entire translation. Levertoff's translation is nothing short of a misrepresentation of the contents and character of the work he supposedly translates. I do not mean that he has skipped passages and translated passages. I mean, the passages he purports to translate are given, at best, in a shoddy précis. This was the level of scholarship in Britain in his time,[1] and it shows us how vastly the group around the

[1]Schwab's French version of the Yerushalmi is no different. He skips the hard passages and does not even say so. I cannot reconstruct in my mind the reasoning behind Levertoff's and Schwab's policy (if it was a policy), nor can I make sense of what they proposed to accomplish. My sense is that, here as in

Soncino projects improved upon what they had inherited. We must regard them as pioneers not only in what they did but in the standard that they brought to the entire labor at hand.

Let me give, by way of example, the whole of *Pisqa 3* to show the full dishonesty of Levertoff's work. I give his representation and translation and then mine (including my brief commentary). The differences will then speak for themselves.

**Levertoff**

3

> *And they should confess their sins which they have done.* That is, in cases like these only the person himself must bring a guilt offering and confess, but not his son. [For instance,[ if one says to another: "Give me back the deposit which I left with thy father," [and that one replies}: "Thou hast not left any deposit." – "I adjure thee!" – and that one says: "Amen," and then he remembered [that the claimant was right], are we to suppose that he is obliged to bring a guilt offering]? [No.] For its says here: "They shall confess their sin which *they* have done."

That, sum and substance, is what we have for *Pisqa 3.* Now here is my version of the same *Pisqa.*

**Neusner**

III:I.1

A. "[And the Lord said to Moses, 'Say to the people of Israel, When a man or woman commits any of the sins that men commit [by breaking faith with the Lord,] and that person is guilty, he shall confess his sin which he has committed, and he shall make full restitution for his wrong, adding a fifth to it, and giving it to him to whom he did the wrong.']" (Num. 5:5-10).

B. But [he does not have to make confession] for what his father did.

C. For if one said to him, "Give me the bailment that I left with your father," and he says, "You left no bailment," [and the other says,] I impose an oath on you," and the first says, "Amen,"

D. [and if] after a while the [son] remembers [that a bailment had been left and must be handed over],

E. should I conclude that he is liable [to make confession and bring the guilt-offering, not merely to hand over the bailment]?

F. Scripture says, " he shall confess his sin which *he* has committed," but he does not make confession for what his father did.

---

most matters of scholarship, people make things up as they go along and do whatever they feel like doing.

The prooftext serves for a proposition given in apodictic form. We shall now derive laws from the verses at hand to cover further such situations.

III:II.1

A. "...and he shall make full restitution for his wrong:"
B. Why is this stated?
C. Since it says, "He shall restore it in full" (Lev. 6:4/5:24), I know only that one has to make restitution of the principle.
D. How do I know about the added fifth?
E. Scripture says, "...and he shall make full restitution for his wrong."

The exegesis moves on to a further detail of the cited verse, once more clarifying the relationship of the law to the Scripture.

III:III.1

A. "...adding a fifth to it, and giving it to him to whom he did the wrong" (Num. 5:5-10):
B. That is on condition that the principle and the added fifth add up to five *selas*.
C. In the name of R. Josiah they said, "It may be even a fifth of a single *sela*."

The proposed condition in no way appears in the verse at hand, so the exegesis consists in bringing to the verse considerations formed outside of it.

III:IV. 1

A. "...adding a fifth to it, and giving it to him to whom he did the wrong." (Num. 5:10):
B. Why is this said?
C. Because it is further said, "...he shall restore it in full and shall add a fifth to it and give it to him to whom it belongs on the day of his guilt offering" (Lev. 6:5/5:25).
D. I know, therefore, that one has to give the compensation to the injured party himself.
E. How do I know that I should apply also to the man's agent, the agent of a court, or the heir?
F. Scripture says, "...adding a fifth to it, and giving it to him to whom he did the wrong." (Num. 5:10) [encompassing these other parties].
G. R. Nathan says, "Lo, if there were a case in which one owed his fellow a hundred [*zuz*], and came to court, but did not suffice to hand over the money before the creditor of the party from whom the money had been stolen came alone [and laid claim on the funds]. How do we know that one has to seize the funds from the

thief and pay them over to the creditor of the one who had been victim of the theft?

H. "Scripture says, '...giving it to him to whom he did the wrong.' (Num. 5:10) – under all circumstances."

Once more we read the language of the verse so as to clarify cases not explicitly covered. The purpose over all is to expound the cited verse with the cases of the law in mind.

We see that Levertoff gives what is in fact only the opening discourse, numbered by me as **III:I**. The rest he not only omits but also ignores. He does not even indicate that he is giving only a piece of the discussion. So the full extent of his abridgement is not made clear. His notes to the passage at hand (p. 7) focus on details of interest to New Testament scholars. In the present passage, he comments after "Amen," as follows: "The usual formula of the acceptance of an oath. *Su eipas* (Matt. xvi 24) is not to be found in rabbinic literature as an affirmative of an oath." The notes are no more informative than the text – except as to the audience Levertoff had in mind. So much for the translation as précis!

Levertoff of course has no reference system worthy of the name. Even though the reader cannot have forgotten the point, let me once more call attention to the inadequacy of the reference system of all former translators (if we can call theirs "reference systems" at all). The reader will have noted an annotation scheme clearly different from Levertoff's. He reproduces the annotation-scheme of the received editions. It consists of numbering the whole units, 1, 2, 3, to the end. I have then subdivided. This I did along two lines. First of all, I number the paragraphs as given in Horovitz. So if at *Pisqa 3* he has four distinct paragraphs, I number them with a roman numeral, added to the numeral covering the pericope as a whole, thus III:I, III:II. Then I subdivided the paragraphs into what seem to me complete and whole discourses, thus III:I.1. Finally, I subdivide these completed discourse into their components, that is, the smallest whole units of thought ("sentences"). This I do with letters, A, B, C, and so on. Accordingly, the entire composite is clearly identified and dissected, so that further studies may readily identify the smallest units of discussion. I have never understood why earlier translators, as well as those who published the critical texts to begin with, did not find it necessary to provide a system for referring to the materials at hand. So much for the translation as précis: it is how people used to do the work. And many still do, though, happily, no academician known to me would present a text in so meretricious a manner as Levertoff did.

# 7

# The Reference Translation: Hammer on Sifré to Deuteronomy

A fine example of a reference translation is Hammer's presentation of Sifré to Deuteronomy. We shall begin with that work, noting its strengths and weaknesses, and then generalize on the promise and problem of that approach to translating the classics of Judaism.[1] In Hammer's version we gain access to the contents, but to no other detail, of Sifré to Deuteronomy. In making my translation I consulted Hammer many times as I prepared my translation and always found his ideas instructive and helpful. Hammer's translation of Sifré to Deuteronomy, based on the Hebrew text of Louis Finkelstein, which bears the English title: *Sifre on Deuteronomy. Published originally by the Gesellschaft zur Foerderung der Wiessenschhaft des Judentums. And now re-published by The Jewish Theological Seminary of America. Through the generosity of the Stroock Publication Fund* (New York, 1969: The Jewish Theological Seminary of America) and B. Kosovsky, *Concordance to the Sifre* (Jerusalem, 1970), makes available in serviceable and clear English an important statement of the Judaism of the Dual Torah concerning Scripture.

What has he done right? The first, and major, strength of Hammer's translation lies in its clear and clean English. He remains exceedingly close to the text, as he should, while giving us ready access to its sense and meaning. I found the English fluent and entirely acceptable. So far as I checked, I found the translation consistently accurate and such minor mistakes as I noted do not detract from the overall solidity and excellence of the work. It is a reliable and

[1]Reuven (né: Robert) Hammer, *Sifre. A Tannaitic Commentary on the Book of Deuteronomy. Translated from the Hebrew with Introduction and Notes.* New Haven and London, 1986: Yale University Press. Yale Judaica Series XXIII.

accurate account, in English, of the Hebrew text. Occasionally I may differ from him, but in the main the differences are trivial.[2]

The second, and also considerable, strength of Hammer's work is his erudite notes. These are mainly philological, amplifying matters of the sense of words or passages. There are cross-references, variant readings, brief philological notes, and the like – all pertinent, valuable, and illuminating. The indexes are useful, though Hammer's references to modern scholarship are not indexed, there is no list of authorities he has consulted, and there is no systematic bibliography.[3] The introduction provides a useful summary of much of the received scholarship on the document. Hammer has not paid any attention at all to the important issues on the literary analysis of Sifré to Deuteronomy raised by Stephen Fraade in his *Hebrew Union College Annual* studies. He seems not to have taken to heart the results of a great many contemporary inquiries into rabbinic literature.[4] Still, as far as it goes, the introduction summarizes much work and therefore is useful and informative.

The translation of Sifré to Deuteronomy was therefore done again, beginning to end, for two reasons. By this point in my exposition of a theory of translation of rabbinic literature, the reader will know what they are. First, Hammer has not supplied the book with even a trace of a usable reference system. Without a clear reference system beyond "Piska 246" that is to say, the mere number of a chapter, no one has any way to indicate to anyone else what is under discussion. The failure is not minor, for, amazingly, Hammer has not even *paragraphed* the text in accord with Western standards. If we want to undertake an analytical study of any passage, we therefore shall have to provide a

---

[2]But Herbert Basser's forthcoming review calls into question these positive judgments of mine.

[3]I found this omission surprising in a work from a press of the standard of Yale University Press, and I do not understand it. But Yale Press in other ways proved not up to the task, as I point out below in a later footnote.

[4]Hammer works in Jerusalem, where the scholarly ethos encourages *Todschweigen*, that is to say, murdering through silence, in concrete terms, not quoting or citing or even considering the ideas of scholars not admitted to the canon of works suitable for quoting, citing, and contending with. As is clear, Hammer has paid a very heavy price for his failure to learn from others; but so do all those of the Jerusalem school and its Western branches, Jewish Theological Seminary of America (on the Jerusalem faculty of which he is a member) and other rabbinical schools, for instance. Scholarship progresses despite the absence of discourse with Jerusalem and those in communication with Jerusalem.

suitable reference system and also reparagraph the entire document. And that means a completely new translation.

In Hammer's defense, I have to point out that two other translations of Sifré to Deuteronomy remain as slavishly tied to the Hebrew mode of paragraphing as does his. The first is Herbert W. Basser, *Midrashic Interpretations of the Song of Moses* (New York, Frankfort on the Main, and Berne, 1984: Peter Lang. *American University Studies.* Series VII. *Theology and Religion.* Volume II). Basser covers *Pisqaot* 306 through 341. He does not supply a reference system, though his paragraphing is somewhat more informative than is Hammer's. The other is Hans Bietenhard, *Sifre Deuteronomium. Uebersezt und erklaert. Mit einem Beitrag von* Henrik Ljungman (New York, Frankfort on the Main, and Berne, 1984: Peter Lang. *Judaica et Christiana.* Ed. Simon Lauer and Clemens Thomas. *Institut für jüdisch-christliche Forschung an der Theologischen Fakultaet Luzern*). Bietenhard's learned and well-annotated translation provided no clear reference system.

Second, Hammer does not give us any indication of the sources upon which the authorship at hand has drawn its materials, or the relationship between what we find in this text and what we find in parallels. This can be done within a translation itself. For example, I always present a verbatim citation of the Mishnah and the Tosefta in bold-face type. The great text-editors, S. Buber and C. Albeck, for example, always provide in footnotes a reasonable picture of the sources that are collected and set forth in a given compilation. By contrast, Hammer's notes are remarkably unclear on these matters. For instance, while he does refer us to (many, though not all) parallels, he does not indicate that the reference to the parallel calls attention to an alternative version or merely to a topically relevant item, one that intersects in some detail with the one at hand. The notes that allude to what he imagines are "parallels" therefore detract from, rather than advance, the inquiry.

For example (chosen at random) at *Piska* 182 N. 2, I am referred to Mak. 2:2, with a comment on the substance of the matter. Hammer does not indicate in the translation that the passage is a verbatim citation of a Mishnah-passage. His reference to Mak. 2:2 (not indicating that it is the Mishnah-tractate) does not tell me whether I have before me a word-for-word citation of Mishnah tractate Makkot or a reference to pertinent information. (In fact, it is the latter.) *Piska* 183 N. 1 has Tos. Mak. 2:1, and so it goes. This is remarkably uninformative. Hammer has given information of limited use. It means that, despite Hammer's elaborate set of notes, anyone who wishes to analyze the text has to redo the entire work of comparing what we have here to what occurs in other documents within the canon of the Judaism of the Dual Torah. My purpose, preparing the way for my introduction, has not required me to redo this part of the work. But anyone who wants to study the uses of diverse materials in various rabbinical compilations of the canon of late antiquity is going to have to undertake it.

So the available translation ignores the opportunity of informing readers where and when the document at hand makes use of, or shares, materials found in other compilations, though Hammer had all that information in hand when he did his work. Hammer also does not allow us to undertake analysis of the types and forms of discourse, the comparison and relationship between one paragraph or chapter with some other, or any other analytical study whatsoever. The translation therefore does not make possible any kind of sustained analytical study. Hammer has made available the contents of the text, but in such a form that one can do virtually nothing with the document, beyond alluding to those contents. He seems to have taken for granted that the only thing readers would do with this translation is consult it for what it says about a given subject or verse of Scripture, and, in the scholarly context of the theological study of ancient Judaic texts by rabbis and theologians, he is assuredly right. But for all other work, the translation has to be done fresh, with the correct analytical presentation to permit a variety of research inquiries.

Now to generalize on the matter. As I have already indicated, because of Hammer's failure to provide an adequate reference system to this document, I had almost immediately to retranslate the entire document.[5] Originally I had not planned to translate the document at all.[6] But for reasons that are now abundantly clear, Hammer's work is useless for any purpose other than reference. Hammer provides a

---

[5]Hammer's translation was supported by the National Endowment for the Humanities. When the work reached me, I communicated with the Division of Research Programs and suggested that when NEH supports scholarly translations, they require the provision of some sort of reference system (beyond commas, periods, and paragraphing). NEH has supported a variety of translations from Hebrew classics, and these have proved uneven in quality. But in the balance the work seems to me to range from marginally competent to good.

[6]In connection with research then underway, I asked to consult Hammer's translation, to find whether materials I was seeking were in that document. But I was denied access to it, even for scholarly purposes, prior to its actually appearing in print. I regret that Yale University Press and its Judaic series as well as Professor Hammer did not wish to facilitate my research; it is a mark of the state of the field of Judaic Studies that that should have been the case. I should have given Yale University Press more credit than that.

generally reliable rendition in English of what the Hebrew says. The reason for undertaking the retranslation and analysis of Sifré to Deuteronomy therefore is simple.

It is the simple fact, therefore, that our present knowledge of the document in any reference translation in English extends only to its contents. If people want to know only what (to speak again of the case at hand) Sifré to Deuteronomy contains, they can look it up in Hammer's translation (or, to be sure, mine). If they want to know what Sifré to Deuteronomy tells us about its authorship and its context, the message it wished to deliver, its judgment upon the larger issues of its setting as the canon of the Judaism of the Dual Torah defines that setting, they will not find answers, composed in accord with the canons of contemporary scholarly inquiry, in any translation before mine. In my translation I prepared the way to provide answers to the questions that can be addressed on the basis of a form-analytical reading of the document. In subsequent studies of course I utilized the analytical system and structure to produce, on the basis of inductive inquiry, answers to the simple questions: What is this book? How does it undertake discourse? What are its salient structural traits? and the like.

Let me explain how and why scholarship on the rabbinic literature up to now has not addressed the simplest questions of definition and analysis in the sole correct way, which is inductive. For one example, is Sifré to Deuteronomy a composite or is it a cogent composition? Is it a sustained and unitary text, or a collection of discrete fragments that someone has thrown together for reasons we cannot imagine? No one has asked that question. Yet if we do not know the answer, we cannot say whether the document makes a statement at all, or whether it simply preserves this and that about whatever. We do not at this point know how to classify the writing even in its fundamental aspect of cogency. For another example, do we deal with a rhetorically and logically cogent document, or do a variety of rules of discourse govern the making of intelligible statements? No one has answered that question. Yet if we do not know how an authorship proposes to engage in intelligible discourse, how can we hear the messages that that authorship proposes not only to declare in so many words but also to convey in all of those other signals of meaning that, in any piece of intelligent writing, convey meaning?

To take yet a third example, since no one has read the document whole and complete and also in the context of other documents, also read as distinctive statements, thus seeing each one whole and distinct, yet canonically related to affines, we have no comparative study to allow us to see what is particular in this writing, what characterizes a number of other writings as well. And that sort of comparison of whole documents to one another has no bearing upon the presence, in two or more compilations, of a few items cited more or less in the same language. So even though we have access to the contents of Sifré to Deuteronomy, we cannot even interpret what we know about the book – the contents essentially unanalyzed, whether in Hebrew or in English.

The correct methodological approach is dictated by established procedures in all humanistic learning in the West. First, we have to allow a document such as Sifré to Deuteronomy to speak for itself. Its authorship's own choices as to aesthetic and substantive questions alike must give their testimony. The choices of that authorship on how to express its ideas constitute the single authoritative commentary to the document.[7] That means the traits of the document demand attention on their own, without an a priori premise as to the origin, purpose, or character of the writing before us. Furthermore, we cannot take at face value what other documents say about it – if they allege anything at all.

It further means we cannot take at face value claims of the authorship itself. That authorship proposes to situate the document within a particular circle of authorities, by claiming, e.g., that a saying was said by a named authority. Knowing when that authority lived – so the authorship assumes – then informs us of the historical and canonical standing of that saying. But we cannot assume without solid evidence that a saying attributed by the authorship before us really was said by that person. That sort of gullibility characterizes no scholarship in the Western tradition. Curiosity, criticism, inquiry – these rest on evidence, not faith. True, the authorship wishes us to believe that it speaks not in its own name but in the name of a variety of identified authorities. It then presents a consensus of the named authorities and their colleagues. That claim is natural and probably necessary. It is what persuaded people to accept the document and to

---

[7]The conception that the medieval commentaries tell us the original meaning of an ancient document need not detain us. When my translations are criticized as ignorant for, e.g., ignoring what Rashi has to say about a passage in the Talmud of Babylonia, I marvel that my intent has registered. For that is not out of "ignorance" but entirely intentional. I began this mode of reading the rabbinic texts with the Mishnah, insisting that the Mishnah constitutes its own best exegesis, and that when people say things in one way and not in some other, that constitutes a signal as to their intent and meaning. I extended that same critical hermeneutics to principal documents of the rabbinic canon, and hope to complete the task. No one doubts that the received exegetical tradition contains points of interest, particularly as to the possible meanings of words and phrases.

preserve and copy, and also believe in it. But the process of description, analysis, and interpretation cannot be limited solely to the information the original authorship provided and the propositions that authorship wishes to establish.

Quite to the contrary, the beginning of criticism is not gullibility but independent analysis, not credence in what people wish us to believe, but sustained inquiry into objective traits of evidence, analysis of the indicative characteristics of that evidence, interpretation through comparison and contrast of the outcome of that analysis and inquiry. The methodological requirements of contemporary humanistic inquiry dictate the empirical approach adumbrated here. That approach has not defined systematic work on Sifré to Deuteronomy as any prior scholar proposing to introduce – that is, describe and define Sifré to Deuteronomy – has done that work.[8]

My generative question is a simple one. If we derive our information only what the writing itself reveals, that is, internal evidence, inductively sifted, what can we say about Sifré to Deuteronomy? That defines that starting point, which we may call ground zero. No introduction to the document, e.g., in an encyclopaedia article or in a prior translation such as Hammer's, starts solely with the data of the writing.[9] All of them begin with allegations as to the character of the document contained with the ancient corpus of rabbinic writings. Everyone takes for granted, for one thing, that all statements attributed to named authorities in the document really were said by those authorities and testify to the character of opinion, now preserved in this writing, held at the time of those authorities. But what if we do not believe as fact everything ancient writers tell us? Then what do we really know about the authorities of the composite, their intentions, their plan and program?

And how do we place into context the result of their work? In beginning from a position of curiosity, but not credulity, I reopen questions long thought settled. For reasons now spelled out, I propose to pursue those questions in a way appropriate to learning today, which is

---

[8]Episodic work on individual passages, by contrast, has some merit, and I am happy at the outset to stipulate that all exegetical work on the meanings of words and phrases provides definitive results, none of which has any material bearing on our problem at all. I take for granted Hammer and those he cites know the meanings of words and phrases. But reviewers of his translation who take a keen interest in these matters do not concur in my positive evaluation of his philological competence.

[9]We shall return to the matter of introducing rabbinic classics. It is not to be divorced from the theory of translation.

to say, by an inductive inquiry into the character of the evidence, and then by a comparative study of the results of inductive inquiry into several comparable documents. In these two processes, I shall say upon an empirical basis what I believe we can conclude about the character and context of the document at hand. Let me now turn to the problem at hand. So much for Hammer's reference translation. We shall presently consider his introduction, which exhibits in an exemplary way the flaws of all introductions to rabbinic classics attached to current translations.

# Part Three
# WHAT IS AT STAKE IN THE ANALYTICAL TRANSLATION

# 8

# What Is at Stake in the Analytical Translation:

## [1] The Problem of the Textual Tradition and the Solution of Form Analysis

The problem of the infirm textual tradition on which almost all scholarship on the classics of Judaism in late antiquity rests is easily set forth. Until we come to medieval times we have no authoritative evidence, in the form of dated manuscripts, for any document of the Judaism of the Dual Torah. We do not know that the entirety of the book that we now call – to take the example that will dominate in this discussion – Sifré to Deuteronomy existed in late antiquity. Manuscript evidence cannot tell us that everything now in hand was there to begin with. What to do? We stand on solid ground in maintaining that the cogent discourse that defines the document's rhetoric, topic, and logic marked the document from its original stages. If people added materials, the established program is what dictated their choices. Otherwise, we should discern not one but a variety of rhetorical, logical, and topical programs. And, as we shall see, if we so translate as carefully to replicate in English the formal traits of these highly formalized writings, we can easily portray the paramount and indicative traits that characterize one document and (comparative study will show) not some other. On that basis we may cope with the insoluble problem of not being able, through manuscript evidence, to recover the "original" version of a document. Let me spell out my reasoning with emphasis upon the formal conventions that predominate in most of the writings under consideration here. The role of translation in making possible the identification of the indicative traits of these formal conventions will remain implicit for the moment.

If we are able to assign the document to a (any) particular point of origination, we gain out of the definitive paradigm of rhetoric, topic, and logic a clear picture of the sustaining position of the authorship at hand *ab origine*. Others, joining the creative work of handing on the document, added what they chose, but as we recognize, solely in line with the established principles of public discourse. It is the uniformity of rhetoric, topic, and logic that justifies the claim to treat the document as cogent, even though later tradents joined the process of formulation and formation.[1] When I propose to relate the indicative traits of the document to the circumstance within the unfolding canon I believe definitive for the document,[2] I refer not to any single *pisqa*, let alone a statement within one, but to the definitive and indicative traits of the whole, logic, rhetoric, topic alike, and these in the larger context of the canonical program of the framers of the Dual Torah in the late fourth, fifth, and sixth centuries.

Why do I regard the analytical translation as essential in solving this problem of the parlous textual tradition for all the rabbinic writings that reach us from late antiquity? The reason is that through making clear the main lines of structure and order, identifying each piece of a composition on its own, we make possible the discovery of the formal preferences of an author or authorship. We can then characterize a document by appeal to the internal evidence that writing on its own provides, and we need not rely only on what an authorship says, but can turn to how the authorship makes its statement. I maintain, and I shall now show, that through proper translation we can make possible a variety of definitive studies of indicative traits of the classic documents.

Let me explain why these considerations prove paramount. By definition a composite document such as any one in the entire corpus of Judaism in late antiquity has no single author. But as a coherent statement in both form and proposition, most documents exhibit a cogent

---

[1]I have worked on this problem in my *From Tradition to Imitation. The Plan and Program of Pesiqta deRab Kahana and Pesiqta Rabbati* (Atlanta: Scholars Press for Brown Judaic Studies, 1987). The way in which medieval compilers did the work of making *yalqutim*, or anthologies, clearly differs from the manner in which the authorships of late antiquity accomplished the work of forming midrash-compilations. But I know of no literary critic or literary historian who has compared the results of the two quite distinct periods of literary creativity, each with its task and policy. Knowing nothing about medieval Judaic literature, I am not able to pursue that line of study.

[2]For example, my *Judaism and Society: The Evidence of the Yerushalmi* (Chicago: University of Chicago Press, 1983), and equivalent studies.

character, therefore derive from a considered set of decisions of a rhetorical, logical, and topical order, and, it follows, come from an authorship, a collectivity of consensus about a given piece of writing. To be sure, we do not know whether that authorship as just now defined flourished for ten days or five hundred years. Historical questions are not readily answered through form analysis.

An analytical translation yields access to rhetoric and logic.[3] When in due course I relate the indicative traits of the document to the circumstance within the unfolding canon I believe definitive for the document, I refer not to any single paragraph (e.g., *pisqa*), let alone a statement within one, but to the definitive and indicative traits of the whole, logic, rhetoric, topic alike, and these in the larger context of the canonical program of the framers of the Dual Torah in the late fourth, fifth, and sixth centuries.

The work of the authorship of Sifré to Deuteronomy (or any other piece of writing we have from antiquity) reaches us only through a long process of copying and recopying. Accordingly, we cannot be certain that the Hebrew version in our hands is the one originally sent into the world by the authorship of the document. If, therefore, we propose to represent the traits of mind and intellect of the authorship responsible for a rabbinic document, we cannot appeal to any one detail, e.g., a given paragraph or pericope. That singleton may or may not have found a place in the original version(s), produced by the authorship that bears responsibility for the writing and that has defined and guaranteed the consensus constituted, to begin with, by the document we are studying. We do not have the original manuscript that stated what the initial authorship wished to say. We do not even come within a millennium of that original authorship.

The state of manuscript evidence, whether rich or impoverished, therefore settles few important questions as to the original intent and statement of the responsible authorship. If we wish to know anything at all about the document as its authorship created it, we have to appeal not to particular statements but to the character of the document as a whole, as evidenced in each and every one of its parts. General and ubiquitous traits of rhetoric and logic can be imitated by later copyist-authors, adding their own message to the document as it passes through their hands. But they cannot be invented – and, by definition, they do represent the intent and plan of the original authorship. Not only so, but we may even appeal to overall traits of the topical plan and program of the document for evidence of the initial program, even

---

[3]In Chapter Ten I show how this is done through the correct shaping of a translation.

though one or another subject or specific proposition cannot be reliably imputed to that original authorship. The way we solve the problem of the parlous character of the manuscript tradition and evidence of any rabbinic document of late antiquity – and every document reaches us only by means of the most dubious manuscript-tradition – is to conduct an analysis of the traits of the whole: what defines in all of the parts the indicative character of rhetoric, logic, and topic? When we can answer those questions, we may "introduce" our document, that is to say, answer such basic questions about the classification and definition of the writing as permit us to understand and make sense of that writing.[4]

So much for critics who argue that until all manuscript evidence has been collated (which critics call "the making of a critical text") no work of description, analysis, and interpretation is possible. The single explicit statement on the matter comes from Peter Schaefer, "Research into Rabbinic Literature: An Attempt to Define the *Status Quaestionis*," *Journal of Jewish Studies* 1986, 37:146-152. This article – in many ways disingenuous, in some, rather pretentious – in no way succeeds in its announced purpose, and its discussion of the matter at

---

[4]We revert to this issue in Chapter Nine. Introduction is a separate problem from representation of formal and logical traits of a document, but only when we can define the governing conventions shall we have a grasp of a document as a whole. As we shall see, when Hammer introduces Sifré to Deuteronomy he explains what the literary genre, Midrash, is (as he sees it), and he also explains some of the details of how midrash-exegesis does its work. That is, he moves from the most general frame of reference, far beyond the limits of the text, to the most detailed, well within the nitty-gritty of sentences, without any attention whatsoever to the document at hand as distinguished from all other writings (if it is to be so distinguished, and in my Introduction, I proved that it is). He has the same problem with the propositional program of the document. He introduces by way of example and episodic remarks, merely paraphrasing a bit of what he finds. He does not compare the sum and substance of the propositional program of this document with that of any other. In other words, the failure to translate with close attention to the particular traits of the document under study also leads to the further incapacity to introduce *this document in particular.* It would be unfair to Hammer to suggest that he alone exhibits these marks of abysmal intellectual failure, when, in fact, they characterize every other translation into English of every rabbinic classic known to me. A glance at the catalogue, in the preface, of books of mine devoted to introducing classics of Judaism, such as Judaism: *The Evidence of the Mishnah, Judaism and Society, The Evidence of the Yerushalmi, Judaism and Scripture: The Evidence of Leviticus Rabbah,* and *Judaism and Story: The Evidence of the Fathers According to Rabbi Nathan,* will show what I think is called for. By the standard I have proposed to set in those introductions, Hammer is not the only failure or even the most interesting one.

hand is uncomprehending and (alas) rather pretentious. But others in less explicit ways have raised the issue, not perceiving that that issue had formed one generative consideration for my defining my work of translation as I have. (The other was the impossibility of demonstrating which attributions to named authorities are valid, which not.) We who now do that work use the best texts we have; when better ones come out, we turn to them. But no claim in this book rests on the priority of one reading over some other. And to my knowledge no story cited in this book exists only in a fragment of the larger manuscript evidence for the document that now contains it.

Critics who mount an argument based on the inadequacy of available textual evidence moreover ignore the stress, in the work done today on the history of religion for Judaism, upon the ubiquitous traits of form, including the formalization of rhetoric, the prevalence of a given (documentary) logic, the recurrence and conventionality of a given (documentary) topical program. No one known to me composes a history of religion, for a Judaism, based on the premise that the texts we now have accurately and in every detail represent the original statement of the initial authorship. Quite to the contrary, it is because of the uncertainty of our textual tradition and its available representation that the entire emphasis lies on uniformities and continuities, within a document, of a given convention in rhetoric, logic, and topic. So much for so translating as to highlight the prevailing and characteristic traits, to the exclusion of particular allusions or references or singleton-examples.

What is at stake in the inquiry? To understand the answer, we have to remind ourselves that while in antiquity books or other important writings, e.g., letters and treatises, bore the name of the author or at least an attribution, e.g., Aristotle's or Paul's name, or the attribution to Enoch or Baruch or Luke, that is not the case for the documents of the Judaism of the Dual Torah. For no document in the canon of Judaism produced in late antiquity, by contrast, is there a named author. No document in that canon contains within itself a statement of a clearcut date of composition, a defined place or circumstance in which a book is written, a sustained and ongoing argument to which we readily gain access, or any of the other usual indicators by which we define the authorship, therefore the context and the circumstance, of a book.

There is a reason for that fact. The purpose of the sages who in the aggregate created the canonical writings of the Judaism of the Dual Torah is served by not specifying differentiating traits such as time, place, and identity of the author or the authorship. The canon – "the one whole Torah of Moses, our rabbi" – presents single books as undifferentiated episodes in a timeless, ahistorical setting: Torah revealed to Moses by God at Mount Sinai, but written down long afterward. That theological conviction about the canon overall denies us information to introduce the book at hand, that is, to say, what it is. Without the usual indicators, then, how then are we to read our document on its own terms, so as to answer the question: what is this book? When, where, why was it written? What does it mean?

Lacking clear answers to these questions, we turn to the evidence – yielded by a careful, analytical translation – that the document does provide: its salient traits of plan and program as intrinsic evidence lays these out. By plan I mean simply the literary traits before us. The intellectual program, so far as we can define it, derives from those same literary traits: from *how* the book's authorship persistently and ubiquitously presents its messages, we hope to learn *what* important points that authorship proposed to impart. So these two go together: form and meaning, structure and sustained polemic. Proposing to define the document at hand, we begin from the outside, with formal traits, and work our way inward, toward the deciphering of the messages contained within those recurrent points of interest and stress, to begin with signified in form. Only by seeing the document whole and all at once shall we gain the rudiments of a definition. Describing and so defining bits and pieces would yield no encompassing description of the whole. If we ask, therefore, what is this book, we begin with the entirety of the document.

If, as we must, we focus on intrinsic traits, exhibited within the words of the document itself, we do not know much more than that the book forms part of a canon of books. That we know because (again using Sifré to Deuteronomy as our example) Sifré to Deuteronomy persistently refers to a book other than itself, specifically, sections of the pentateuchal and prophetic writings of the Hebrew Scriptures ("Old Testament"). But the selection of the sections chosen for treatment, specified on the table of contents, conforms to no clear pattern and so cannot find explanation by reference to some larger task or plan. For some of the passages derive from the Pentateuch, some from the prophetic books, and at least two of the *pisqaot* do not, to begin with, refer to verses of Scripture at all. Still the fact that the authorship declares its dependence upon another authorship – a fact deriving from entirely intrinsic traits, inductively discovered – testifies to the canonical context in which our document comes into being. In point of fact, all we know about any complete piece of writing, with a beginning, middle, and end we can discern, is that it forms a document organized around another document, that is, in conventional language, it is a commentary to a text. But that observation requires considerable qualification and revision, when we note that the text to which our document persistently refers and therefore forms a commentary turns out not to be Scripture at all.

What does that mean? Simply this: were we to approach our document without the knowledge that the authors take as their point of departure – organization and formal program of their book – an already-available text – if not Scripture as such – written by someone else, we should understand very little in the book at hand. Any rabbinic text read out of alignment with the generative text of its choice (as yet unspecified) presents unintelligible gibberish. To state matters affirmatively, we define the present book only when we can describe its relationship to the text that forms the trellis for its vine. But once we know that in hand is a commentary to a text, we still possess little more knowledge of the program and purpose of a rabbinic document than we did prior to our observing that simple fact. For (to revert to the list of things we do not know) we still do not know who wrote the book, for what purpose, with the intent of advancing what ideas or program. We do not even know what made the authorship select as the organizing structure for its book the text that it chose in particular, or whether some other text – mode of organizing ideas and attaching them to a common structure and pattern – would have served his purpose just as well.

The extrinsic traits of the document at hand tell us practically nothing about the book and do not permit us to define it. So we cannot say what a rabbinic writing is and is not, who wrote it, to make what point, when, why, where, and on and on. And if we cannot answer these questions, we also cannot make sense of the document before us. We know what it says, but we do not know what it means. Lacking all context, any document of Judaism provides a set of merely formal observations. We simply do not know what the book is, even though we can say what is in the book (and even define the meanings of words and phrases in the interstices of discourse). But where shall we look to find a context for description? The answer is the internal traits. The sole fact in hand is the document itself. For even the context – the canonical setting – is imputed by others, by circumstance and sentiment beyond the pages of the book.

My insistence upon an inductive reading of internal evidence and that alone defines the next stage in the argument. This requires me first to classify, then to specify the internal evidence of choice. The evidence of a document of late antiquity will fall into three classifications: rhetoric, recurrent modes or patterns of expression; topic, the program of systematic exposition of a limited number of themes; and logic, the principle that joins one sentence to the next in an intelligible proposition or syllogism and that imparts cogency and integrity to the document in each of its parts and as a whole. A proper analytical translation will highlight the rhetoric and give access to the logic as well. No other mode of translation will do so. But only when we have a clear picture of the implications of the document's own traits of plan and program may we move beyond the limits of the writing and ask about the context in which the document at hand finds its location.

Among the three definitive or indicative traits of a piece of sustained writing, rhetoric, logic, and topic, the first is the easiest to characterize, since it is, by definition, recurrent and repetitive. The logic or principle of cogent discourse, which imparts (in the mind of the authorship) intelligibility comes to formal expression in rhetoric, so we commonly move from description of rhetoric to analysis of the logical foundations of rhetoric. And, under normal circumstances, the third and most difficult point of entry into a definition of the document is its topical program. For that is in the nature of things diffuse, since the authorship treats more than a single topic, and it is, furthermore, the indicative trait of the document least likely to form connections to other documents, authorships' preferring, after all, to say something fresh or at least something old in a new way. But if we propose to analyze the rhetoric of a document, then our translation (or edition of the text in its original language) must highlight the traits of rhetoric. The available translation does not do so, which is why, alas, we have to retranslate the book, beginning to end. Still, anyone who understands the intellectual glories of the rabbinic literature will not regret the occasion to do so. The stakes are considerable: access to the intellects of those who founded Judaism as we know it. Our pilgrimage calls us from text, to (literary) context, to (cultural) matrix. The road is marked by those forms and modes of discourse that are highlighted, whether in the Hebrew and Aramaic or in translation into Modern Hebrew or English, Spanish, Italian, German, or Portuguese, through the discipline of the analytical translation, and through the provision of a decent reference system. Some half a millennium after the Hebrew Scriptures were given their reference system, it seems to me about time to make possible a labor of intellect other than the work of citation and paraphrase that, until our own day, has passed for scholarship on the history of Judaism in late antiquity. I did the work the way I did because I had no choice.

# 9

# What Is at Stake in the Analytical Translation:

## [2] The Problem of Introducing a Classic Text

How are we supposed to introduce a piece of writing, if we cannot say anything definitive about that particular piece of writing? Take, for instance, the problem of writing an encyclopaedia article about a rabbinic classic, for one established way in which we state the knowledge that we have concerning a given text is to write an encyclopaedia article. But were we to face the task of writing an encyclopaedia article on a given document – once more, I take as my case Sifré to Deuteronomy, – we should address a set of questions to which, at this time, we do not have answers. For example, we should want to answer these questions:

[1] where, when, and by whom was the book written?
[2] what is the book about?
[3] does the author propose to argue a particular case, and, if so,
[4] what polemic does he propose to advance?
[5] as to literary classification, is this writing a book or a scrapbook, a cogent statement or a composite?

Defining the document demands classifying it, and that means we must compare and contrast the document with others of its kind. Describing the document requires stating its main indicative traits and points of emphasis. In other words, just what *is* Sifré to Deuteronomy, what *sort* of a book is it, and what particular example of *that* sort of book is it? These questions define the work of introducing a book – any book. The answers to these and other questions constitute the definition of our book as of any other. They tell us *what it is,* meaning its character as a piece of sustained writing, context, composition, and contents. To introduce (to take our case at hand) Sifré to Deuteronomy, we should therefore compose a systematic response to an established set of questions of definition. We should begin, then, with the question of the author: who wrote the book (or compiled it), where, why, when, for what audience. Legitimate questions all, none of them can be answered on the basis of evidence internal to a single writing in the canon of Judaism.

The reason is a powerful theological position that works against the signing of books by named authors, on the one side, and the delineation of the traits of one document as distinct from all others, on the other side. These two traits mean that all work must be inductive and all evidence internal. The question of authorship is primary. All classics of the Judaism of the Dual Torah exhibit one definitive characteristic. It is that none is signed by a named author or is so labeled (except in a few instances long after the fact) as to represent the opinion of a lone individual. In their intrinsic traits of discourse all speak out of the single, undifferentiated voice of Sinai, and each makes a statement of the Torah of Sinai and within that Torah. That anonymity, indicative for theological reasons, poses problems for the historian of religious literatures. For it denies us that knowledge of place, time, and circumstance of composition that permits us to relate contents to context, setting to substantive discourse, and so to interpret a religious system in its social situation, one principal task of the history of religion including its literature. The result for the history of literature of the Judaism of the Dual Torah presents an equivalent obstacle. And that fact explains the problem of introducing a classic of the Judaism of the Dual Torah.

We really do not know who wrote anything, where, when, or why, and so find the literary-critical interpretation of a given document as parlous as the study of that same document within the history of the religious system to which it partially testifies. And, it goes without saying, the use of that same document for the study of history – that is, the history of the nation that produced and preserved that writing – faces equivalent obstacles. When a piece of writing contains no explicit internal evidence about who wrote it, for what reason, in what place and time, to solve what problem, the appeal to that document for the history of religion, for the interpretation of literature, and for the study of history, produces only muffled echoes but few clear notes.

Such authors as (the school of) Matthew or Luke, Josephus, even the writer(s) of Ezra-Nehemiah, will have found such a policy of anonymity surprising. And while Socrates did not write, Plato and Aristotle did – and they signed their own names (or did the equivalent in context). In antiquity books or other important writings, e.g., letters and treatises, ordinarily, though not always, bore the name of the author or at least an attribution, e.g., Aristotle's or Paul's name, or the attribution to Enoch or Baruch or Luke. For no document in the canon of Judaism produced in late antiquity, by contrast, is there a named author in the document. No document in that canon contains within itself a statement of a clearcut date of composition, a defined place or circumstance in which a book is written, a sustained and ongoing argument to which we readily gain access, or any of the other usual indicators by which we define the authorship, therefore the context and the circumstance, of a book.

But the authorship[1] of Sifré to Deuteronomy has permitted answering none of these questions about who they were. (Nor does any other authorship of a classic of Judaism of the Dual Torah brought to closure in late antiquity allow us to answer them either.) For internal evidence hardly permits speculation on the circumstance of composition or the purpose of publication. True enough, modern scholarship has presented a sizable corpus of answers to these questions. But until now, scholars have taken attributions of sayings at face value, so that if the text alleges that a given set of sages made the statements at hand, then scholars assume the book was written by, or in the circle and time of, those sages. That is pure gullibility. If, further, a stray-saying alleges that Rabbi X stands behind document Q (e.g., the Tosefta belongs to Hiyya, the Mishnah to Judah the Patriarch), then of course we know that the Mishnah comes from the time and circle of Judah, whatever is not given a name but appears anonymously then bears the approval and authority of Judah the Patriarch, and so for the Tosefta.[2] Once we enter the world of critical learning and ask the ineluctable questions of the critical agenda, we look to internal evidence for validation or invalidation of all statements such as those concerning authorship and circumstance.

So if we insist that internal evidence, and that alone, defines the character of a document, then the available speculation, while

---

[1]This matter is treated in Chapter Eight but is important in this chapter as well. By definition a composite document such as ours has no single author. But it exhibits a cogent character, therefore derives from a considered set of decisions of a rhetorical, logical, and topical order, and, it follows, derives from an authorship, a collectivity of consensus about this particular writing.

[2]Readers who think I exaggerate the gullibility of the paramount school of scholarship on these writings under rabbinical auspices should immediately turn to the Appendix, where Hammer, who teaches in the Jerusalem branch of the Jewish Theological Seminary of America, displays every premise I have catalogued here (and then some!).

imaginative and engaging, does not mark the end to research on this document – or scarcely even the beginning. Not only so, but the questions that we do ask must prove congruent with the character of the solid information in our hands; what the text as we now have it does not tell us, we cannot ask. Our program of inquiry must correspond to the character of the data that we sift. That accounts for the foci of my introduction. There I introduced three matters, all of them, as a matter of fact, exceedingly well documented in the recurrent structures and modes of this writing: rhetoric, logic, topic.[3] I cannot think of simpler questions than those of describing, analyzing, and then interpreting through systematic comparisons, the most superficial traits of the writing before us. Accordingly, the questions under discussion here, involving as they do not the history of manuscripts but the character of the document itself, await attention on the basis of the internal evidence itself, and to do so I have devised methods for both translation, highlighting the pertinent traits, and then survey and analysis.

We turn to the theological reason for the anonymity of the writings of the canon of the Judaism of the Dual Torah. I believe that absolutely fundamental proposition forms the premise of the entire canon of the Judaism of the Dual Torah. Books such as Sifré to Deuteronomy that after formulation were accepted as part of the canon of Judaism, that is, of "the one whole Torah of Moses our rabbi revealed by God at Sinai," ordinarily do not contain answers to questions of definition that commonly receive answers within the pages of a given book because once a piece of writing becomes canonical, by definition it loses all traits of documentary specificity and enters the undifferentiated status of "Torah," that is, God's revelation to Israel. Within revelation, the Torah, there are no boundaries of space or time ("no prior or posterior in the Torah" is a well-established, hermeneutical principle, for instance), and, with God the author of everything true, no reason to identify the limits of one author's contribution and to specify the particular contribution of some other. Everything is Torah, every sentence forms part of an undifferentiated whole, without regard to the frontiers marked by the beginnings and endings of distinctive writings.

The theological purpose of the sages who in the aggregate created the canonical writings of the Judaism of the Dual Torah therefore is served by *not* specifying differentiating traits such as time, place, and

[3]In Chapter Ten I show how the manner in which we translate makes possible the accomplishment of the description of the first two of these three bodies of indicative traits.

identity of the author or the authorship. The canon – "the one whole Torah of Moses, our rabbi" – presents single books as undifferentiated episodes in a timeless, ahistorical setting: Torah revealed to Moses by God at Mount Sinai, but written down long afterward. That theological conviction about the canon overall means to deny us information to introduce the book at hand, that is, to say, what it is. Without the usual indicators, then, how are we to read our document on its own terms, so as to answer the question: what is this book? When, where, why was it written? What does it mean?

Lacking clear answers to these questions therefore explains why, in my definition of the work of introduction, we turn to the evidence the document does provide: its salient traits of plan and program as intrinsic evidence lays these out. By plan I mean simply the literary traits before us. The intellectual program, so far as we can define it, derives from those same literary traits. That is to say, from the rhetoric and logic, the *how* that defines the way the book's authorship persistently and ubiquitously presents its messages, we hope to learn the *what,* that is, the important points that authorship proposed to impart. These two go together: form and meaning, structure and sustained polemic. Proposing to define the document at hand, we begin from the outside, with formal traits, and work our way inward, toward the deciphering of the messages contained within those recurrent points of interest and stress, to begin with signified in form. Only by seeing the document whole and all at once shall we gain the rudiments of a definition. Describing and so defining bits and pieces would yield no encompassing description of the whole. If we ask, therefore, what is this book, we begin with the entirety of the document. And then we turn to other documents of the same classification to see what is special to ours.

If, however, we focus on intrinsic traits, exhibited within the words of the document itself, we do not know much more than that the book forms part of a canon of books. That we know because Sifré to Deuteronomy persistently refers to a book other than itself, specifically, sections of the pentateuchal and prophetic writings of the Hebrew Scriptures ("Old Testament"). But the selection of the sections chosen for treatment may conform to no clear pattern and so cannot find explanation by reference to some larger task or plan. Still the fact that the authorship declares its dependence upon another authorship – a fact deriving from entirely intrinsic traits, inductively discovered – testifies to the canonical context in which our document comes into being. In point of fact, all we know about a midrash-compilation, e.g., Sifré to Deuteronomy, is that it forms a document organized around another document; that is, in conventional language, it is a commentary to a text. But our analysis of both rhetoric and logic will show us that that simple statement conceals considerable complexities.

True, we define a book only when we can describe its relationship to the text that forms the trellis for its vine. But once we know that in hand is a commentary to a text, we still possess little more knowledge of the program and purpose of (to speak of our example) Sifré to Deuteronomy than we did prior to our observing that simple fact. While it is true that the "commentary form," consisting of the citation of a clause of a verse, followed by a brief phrase in amplification of that clause, forms the elementary building block of rhetoric and the fundamental frame of structure, these elementary forms of our document also prove primitive and inchoate. Not only so, but the primitive form conceals the presence of two utterly discrete logics, one propositional in its cogency, the other not at all propositional in joining two or more sentences into sense-units. So "commentary form" will present us with many traps. And even though we know that we deal with something that, in some ways, looks like a commentary to a text, we still do not know who wrote the book, for what purpose, with the intent of advancing what ideas or program. We do not even know what made the authorship select as the organizing structure for its book the text that it chose in particular, or whether some other text – mode of organizing ideas and attaching them to a common structure and pattern – would have served his purpose just as well. We remain incapable of stating the document's fundamental propositions, its purpose (if it has a purpose) and its program (if it is more than simply to collect this and that about a text that alone imparts cogency to the collection).

What follows? It is that the *extrinsic* traits of the document tell us practically nothing about the book or permit us to define it. So we cannot say what a book such as Sifré to Deuteronomy is and is not, who wrote it, to make what point, when, why, where, and on and on. And if we cannot answer these questions, we also cannot make sense of the document before us, by which I mean, place the statement of the writing into its setting, relate its contents to its context. We know what it says, but we do not know what it means. And that makes the work of introduction rather complicated. Lacking all context, a document such as Sifré to Deuteronomy provides a set of merely formal observations. We simply do not know what the book is, even though we can say what is in the book (and even define the meanings of words and phrases in the interstices of discourse). But where shall we look to find a context for description? The answer is the internal traits. The sole fact in hand is the document itself. For even the context – the canonical setting – is imputed by others, by circumstance and sentiment beyond the pages of the book. These facts govern the character of our work of translation as much as of introduction.

It now is time for me to turn to the internal evidence of a given document of the Judaism of the Dual Torah and to ask its authorship for guidance on what they proposed to accomplish in their composition. My insistence upon an inductive reading of internal evidence, and that alone, defines the next stage in the argument. This requires me first to classify, then to specify the internal evidence of choice. The evidence of a document of late antiquity will fall into three classifications:

[1] rhetoric, recurrent modes or patterns of expression;
[2] logic, the principle that joins one sentence to the next in an intelligible proposition or syllogism and that imparts cogency and integrity to the document in each of its parts and as a whole;
[3] topic, the program of systematic exposition of a limited number of themes.

The first of these two matters, rhetoric and logic, pertain to how we translate, since our translation can make accessible the paramount choices worked out by an authorship. What is required is to translate with due attention to the recurrent syntactic forms chosen by an authorship. The mode of translation likewise makes possible a definition of the distinctive logical program of a piece of writing as well.

Since I have already described the rhetorical and topical programs of a number of canonical documents of the same classification, moreover, I am able to compare the traits of this writing with those of others and to identify those traits that are shared and those that are particular and therefore speak for a particular and distinct authorship. I have likewise done enough work on the logical repertoire selected by a variety of authorships to compare and contrast the choices made by one document's authorship with those characteristic of another document's writers.[4] When our translation gives us a clear picture of the implications of the document's own traits of plan and program we may readily move beyond the limits of the writing and ask about the context in which the document at hand finds its location. These three classifications of information are dealt with, successively, in my

---

[4]See my *The Making of the Mind of Judaism.* Atlanta, 1987: Scholars Press for Brown Judaic Studies. and also *The Formation of the Jewish Intellect. Making Connections and Drawing Conclusions in the Traditional System of Judaism.* Atlanta, 1988: Scholars Press for Brown Judaic Studies.

analytical introduction to a variety of the classics of Judaism, Mekhilta, Sifra, and the two Sifrés, for instance.

Among the three definitive or indicative traits of a piece of sustained writing, rhetoric, logic, and topic, the first is the easiest to characterize through the manner in which we translate, since it is, by definition, recurrent and repetitive. Rhetoric rules through repetition and public adherence. Otherwise all we have is poetry, for the powerful phrase, and idiosyncrasy, for the author of the phrase. The logic or principle of cogent discourse, that is, the way in which one makes a connection between one sentence and another sentence in order to form a sense-unit that transcends them both, is what imparts (in the mind of the authorship) intelligibility. That matter very commonly comes to formal expression in rhetoric, so we move from description of rhetoric to analysis of (what may well prove to form) the logical foundations of rhetoric. That is why I maintain the position outlined here: how we translate also governs the way in which we introduce a text.

Topic is another matter, and here I see no way in which the mode of translation assists in our forming an introduction to a piece of writing. For topic is in the nature of things diffuse, since the authorship treats more than a single topic,[5] and it is, furthermore, the indicative trait of the document least likely to form connections to other documents, authorships' preferring, after all, to say something fresh or at least something old in a new way. Facts of rhetorical form do not require a subjective judgment, and how sentences coalesce to make cogent statements is something for which factual evidence is available, as I shall show. The topical program is another matter entirely, something we can hope to describe only when we have understood how the document makes its statements. Introducing a translation of a given document requires close study of the topical program only in the context of comparison and contrast with other documents; otherwise we are left to paraphrase what the reader has in hand anyhow.

Since, as I said at the outset, by definition a composite document such as ours has no single author nor even an authorship of a determinate time and place that we can identify, my task is dictated for me by the givens of contemporary learning. It is to ask whether this writing exhibits a cogent character and shows conformity to laws and regularities, therefore derives from a considered set of decisions of a rhetorical, logical, and topical order. If it does, then, as a matter of definition, it derives from an authorship, a collectivity that stands

---

[5]Hammer was puzzled about how to handle this matter, so, predictably, he paraphrased. I give a good sample of the paraphrase in the Appendix.

behind the exhibited consensus in this particular writing. Accordingly, if I can find regularities of rhetoric, logic, and topical program, I claim to discern the consequences of rules people – an authorship – have made, decisions they have reached, concerning the character of this writing of theirs: its structure, organization, proposition, cogent statement.[6] If I find no regularities and indications of an orderly program, then I may fairly claim that this writing is different from one that speaks in behalf of people who have made rules or adopted them for the inclusion of fresh ideas of their own. It belongs in a classification not of a composition but of a scrapbook, not of a collage, which uses fixed materials in a fresh way, let alone of a sustained statement of a single system, but of a mishmash of this and that that fell together we know not how.[7]

The return to Hammer's work, by way of contrast, proves anticlimactic. Yet it is required, for how a translator introduces the translation forms part of the intellectual task at hand. We may well predict the character of introductions on the basis of the evidence of the theory of translation. An observation that some chapters back may have proved unintelligible should now enjoy the status of self-evidence: the introduction to a reference translation will attend to the contents of a document, an analytical translation's introduction will raise other questions altogether. To show what is at stake in the theory of translation that guides the work, we glance here at Hammer's introduction to his translation. For the sake of fairness to him, I reproduce in the appendix to this book a sizable part of the whole, leaving out only pages of examples of a single point. Then I turn to the definition of what is required for an introduction to a rabbinic classic rendered into English.

The main characteristic of Hammer's introduction to the document is easily predicted: he will talk about the writings as a whole (midrash in general) and about particulars chosen more or less at random (each meant to exemplify something we are never given in generalization). But there will be no discussion of this document in particular because Hammer does not read this document in particular by reference to any traits that are distinctive to it or indicative of its definitive characteristics. His translation does not show him such

---

[6]To be sure, we do not know – and probably never shall know – whether an authorship, as just now defined, flourished for ten days or five hundred years.

[7]I do make provision for the possibility that what looks to me like a mishmash in fact conforms to rules of cogent discourse I cannot perceive. That possibility is explored in the discussion of the rules of cogency and intelligibility in my *The Making of the Mind of Judaism.*

indicative traits. His failure to compare what he finds here with what he finds elsewhere (the problem of his slovenly references to other writings he deems parallel in some way or another) denies him access to systematic comparison of one writing's contents with those of another writing. This is what I mean when I insist that how we translate dictates also the manner in which we shall introduce a document.

Predictably, at the outset Hammer focuses upon what he calls "the genre of Tannaitic Midrash." I am not quite sure what he means by "genre," or how the adjective "Tannaitic" pertains, or what he means by "Midrash." But these matters scarcely draw us closer to the book he is introducing, since he treats the topic in general terms, not with close reference to the document under study. He turns to what he thinks is an account of the "origin" of this book, but readers may enjoy greater success than I did in locating Hammer's theory of the origin of Sifré to Deuteronomy. All I find is a collection of information on who refers to the book, the sections of the book, and the like. Readers who turn to the appendix will rapidly realize that Hammer's discussion of Goldberg's ideas does not constitute an account of the "origin" of the work. The whole section is garbled and formless. Hammer enjoys greater success in composing his account of "interpretive methods and formulas," though he does not claim that these are particular to this piece of writing; quite to the contrary, he takes for granted that they are not. But then we do not have a sizable account of all of the writings of which this document forms an integral part (these writings that are "basically from the School of R. 'Aqiba"!). But then Hammer believes whatever he finds alleged about this writing; without that gullibility this entire section of his discussion is not possible; as it is, it seems rather implausible. His catalogue of formulaic words and phrases, which I have drastically abbreviated, adds nothing beyond what he says he provides: examples of this and that. The rest of the introduction is paraphrastic and descriptive. One cannot call it a well-crafted piece of thought.

Now let us conclude by asking what an introduction should accomplish. When I wrote my introduction to the same work,[8] my purpose was to present Sifré to Deuteronomy in two ways, first by describing the book in accord with the indicative categories I deem pertinent to an inductive and systematic description; second by cursorily comparing the book to other books of its classification. To introduce the work I ask what is special about it, and I turn to rhetorical and logical

---

[8]*Sifré to Deuteronomy. An Introduction to the Rhetorical, Logical, and Topical Program.* Atlanta, 1987: Scholars Press for Brown Judaic Studies.

traits; in my introduction I am able to show that the descriptive traits of rhetoric and topic that I set forth are not routine, are not merely characteristic of the literature as a whole, but in some particular way to this authorship and the choices it has made. The issue of what is common to the canonical writings under study, and what is particular to this document, is addressed as well.

It is because I had already translated the document in an analytical manner, so highlighting the literary traits of rhetoric and logic of the original that I could introduce it in these terms. In that way I made possible an introduction of the sort that I composed. But my mode of translating was meant to make possible an inductive inquiry into the document's traits of rhetoric, logic, and topic; in the very act of translation, therefore, I describe the indicative traits of the document. Second, in my introduction, through comparative study of Sifré to Deuteronomy and other rabbinic compilations of scriptural exegesis, I propose to situate the document in its larger literary and theological context.[9] Here how we translate seems to me to matter, since a coherent policy of translation will allow us to compare a variety of discrete writings. On that basis, in my introductions to various rabbinic classics, I conduct comparisons between a given document and others generally acknowledged to share its basic point of origin, e.g., Sifra and Sifré to Numbers, as well as other canonical affines, such as Genesis Rabbah, Leviticus Rabbah, and Pesiqta deRab Kahana.[10] In that way I propose to discover what is particular to the composition at hand, and what is shared by that document with others of its species and even of its genus. That, too, is part of the work of introducing a classic of Judaism. To that work, the theory of translation proves critical. But how do we so translate as to expose the main beams of rhetorical and logical structure that sustain and support a document? I shall now give the answer to that fundamental question.

---

[9]The absence of systematic comparative work in Hammer's introduction will strike the reader who looks with care at the abstract given in the Appendix.

[10]I neglected other documents which I have translated whole or in part, such as the Mishnah, Tosefta, Yerushalmi, and Bavli because they are generally deemed to fall into a different classification from the so-called midrash compilations.

# 10

# What Is at Stake in the Analytical Translation:

## [3] Displaying a Document's Rhetoric and Logic

Translation forms the initial act of inquiry, and how we translate will govern the formation of all our questions. To state the theory requires an account of what we see when we translate in the analytical model and miss if we do not. The case for the analytical translation is simply stated. If we do not distinguish one thing from the next, we shall not know two things: first, that some passages resemble others or are unlike others, and, second, that the question of the connection between two or more contiguous passages must be answered. If everything is represented as one thing, that labor of comparison and contrast by definition cannot be done. And the upshot is equally simply stated. If we do not translate with close attention to recurrent formal and syntactic patterning of language and of thought, then we shall not realize that our texts are highly formalized, and that the forms prove a principal medium of thought and expression for our authorships.

Accordingly, everything depends upon the systematic and orderly character of our translation, in which the same things are represented in the same way all of the time and each thing is differentiated from all other things[1] Then what questions can we answer if we do translate analytically and through careful differentiation of units of thought and composites of thought? One question is, do we deal with a

[1]Goldin's highly literary translation obscures the forms of The Fathers According to Rabbi Nathan; his failure to discern the correct divisions of thought, e.g., where paragraphs start and finish, where propositions begin and end, led him to ask questions that were no questions, and to ignore problems that prove blatant. Of Hammer nothing needs to be said.

rhetorically and logically cogent document, or do a variety of rules of discourse govern the making of intelligible statements? No one has answered that question either. Yet if we do not know how an authorship proposes to engage in intelligible discourse, how can we hear the messages that that authorship proposes not only to declare in so many words but also to convey in all of those other signals of meaning that, in any piece of intelligent writing, convey meaning?

But, in general, people study passages in texts, not whole texts, beginning, middle, and end. The result is that, before me, no one has systematically and carefully read whole documents and compared them with other whole documents. That is to say, it is difficult to find in the received tradition of scholarship, both in the yeshiva world and in the seminary world, studies of a given document, presented whole and complete *and also seen in the context of other documents,* also read as distinctive statements. It follows that seeing each one whole and distinct, yet canonically related to affines, represents a new vision. That explains also why, before my introductions of a comparative order, we have no comparative study to allow us to see what is particular in this writing, what characterizes a number of other writings as well. And that sort of comparison of whole documents to one another has no bearing upon the presence, in two or more compilations, of a few items cited more or less in the same language.

So even though we have access to the contents of a given document, we cannot even interpret what we know about that one book. As we see in the exemplary case of Hammer, the contents are left essentially unanalyzed, whether in Hebrew or in English or in any other language. The hopelessness of paraphrase and précis as media of description hardly requires more demonstration than Hammer's hapless Introduction (in the Appendix) provides for us.

## I. Translation and the Representation of Rhetoric

Analytical translation allows us systematically to describe the rhetoric of a document and to compare that document's authorship's choices with the preferences of another writing's authorship. Why does rhetoric matter? Rhetoric is what tells an author how to compose sentences, paragraphs, and chapters, in such a way as to yield an intelligible, cogent, and – above all – persuasive statement. An important component of rhetoric, in the literature at hand, is patterned speech or form. Properly translated, a document will show us its patterns. But precisely what do we seek to locate through the utilization of disciplined and patterned language in English for language of the same type in Hebrew? This requires a definition of forms and the formalization of thought in writing.

Forms comprise fixed, syntactic arrangements of words in which the syntactic pattern is independent of all meaning. Rhetoric, encompassing formalized arrangements of words, of course may derive from individual choice and preference as much as from conventions of a public order. But, as I have explained, the rules of rhetoric within a given document of the Judaism of the Dual Torah stand for, and therefore characterize, the consensus of the community comprised by the authorship of the document. The highly restricted repertoire of syntactic patterns utilized by an authorship of a document in that canon defines an indicative characteristic of the canon and serves a purpose far beyond aesthetic expression. Quite to the contrary, formalized speech as the medium conveys an important component of the message of every document equally. That is why, if we wish to define a document in the canonical literature of the Judaism at hand, we turn first of all to the medium, in language, that everywhere bears the deepest message of the document. Formalized patterns of language constitute the constant indicator of that message.

For, as we noted earlier in this book, no document in the canon of the Judaism of the Dual Torah contains within itself the marks of an individual, and recognized, author. All of them exhibit the traits of a consensus concerning how all matters are to be formulated and expressed. An authorship can say anything – but, in a patterned language, only in a few ways. Within the rules of intelligible speech of the canon, the authorship must choose among those few ways for everything it wishes to convey. The reason is simple. The publication of a book without a named author and without traits of individuality imparted by a known individual or – it must follow – characteristic of an individual and not of shared and public speech, of course, serves an important purpose. The restrictive covenant of speech, the limited repertoire of language – these are meant to secure for the book the standing of the authority of the community as a whole. What speaks for one person bears his name – but then enjoys only his authority as an individual. What speaks for everyone and in the language-conventions of all, then bears no name.

That is why named legal opinions carry no authority, and it is also why the canonical writings carry no evidence of individual hands. The absence of a distinctive author's taste and judgment therefore is conveyed in an aesthetic way as well, for, as we understand now, the medium not only suits, but also forms part of, the message. Accordingly few documents contain extensive marks that a private person's choices of style – how to say things, as much as what to say – dictate the characteristic of the document as a whole. On the contrary, a certain uniformity of style imparts to sayings attributed to individuals a prevailing sameness, consistency in all matters but specific opinion on a single matter. Here, too, we see how a given authorship obliterates the marks of private taste and personal judgment and gains for all of its participants that authority and standing that only the collectivity – the consensus of the group – can supply. But the simple fact is that documents' authorships do make distinctive choices on questions of form, and translations can represent these forms in such a way that we can catalogue the choices of one authorship and compare those choices with the preferences of another authorship.

The fact that writings derive from collective consensus explains the importance of the analysis of the formal traits of a document's rhetoric. Specifically, all rabbinic writings produced in late antiquity closely adhere to repeated forms, literary conventions, and none makes room for or expresses individual preferences as to style and aesthetics. The single, persistent, literary trait of all documents of the canon of the Judaism of the Dual Torah is the highly formalized character of those writings. Set patterns of rhetoric, sentence structure, syntax, word choice, and the like, dominate throughout any given document. These patterns, of course, vary from one document to the next. What matters is that the patterning of language and syntax runs uniformly throughout. That makes it possible for us readily to compare one document to another and to ask how a later authorship has responded to the choices of form made by an earlier one.

I therefore claim that a given document in the aggregate forms one thing of many things. An authorship imposes a limited program of thought and rhetoric, logic and cogency, upon diverse matters. A canonical document of Judaism commonly (though not invariably), therefore, constitutes not a scrapbook but a composition. It rests upon a variety of prevailing indicative traits. Anyone can repeat the procedures I have devised and produce essentially the same result. My care in delineating the outlines of forms, through the utilization of paragraphing in the way indicated, has made possible that repeated recovery of a single result. At each point I have aimed at exemplary results which can be replicated. Form analysis, aimed at identifying recurrent syntactic and other language-patterns and assessing the proportion of the whole dominated by those patterns, requires mere description. If I am right that an authorship finds its choices dictated by a limited repertoire of linguistic conventions, then I should be able to specify precisely what those conventions were and to demonstrate, through a complete survey of the document, that they do indeed predominate throughout. I have in fact done so for all of the documents that I have translated. Let me give a sample of the results. Since I have focused upon Sifré to Deuteronomy, the forms of that document will serve as the source of our examples of forms.

If I may organize and summarize the findings of fixed forms of rhetoric as these concern Sifré to Deuteronomy, we may distinguish all units of thought by a simple criterion. Some units of thought contain generalizations, principles or propositions that bear implications beyond the statement of fact, and others do not. Generalizations, e.g., philosophical propositions, may be stated in a variety of ways. These encompass [1] syllogistic argument; [2] lists of classified facts, in the form of exegesis, that point toward a given proposition or generalization; [3] a particularization of a proposition, followed by a narrative (parable) that restates the proposition in highly general terms; and [4] lists of meanings imputed to a single clause or verse, all of them pointing toward a single conclusion of a general or propositional character. These ways of proving a point have in common an interest in stating not solely a fact but the proposition, e.g., the conclusion the authorship wishes us to draw. That is then the proposition, implicit or otherwise, to be drawn from that fact (or set of facts). Units of thought that bear no proposition, implicit or otherwise, beyond themselves contain a simple statement of fact. All such units of thought adhere to the exegetical form in its primitive state. The fact is deemed to bear its own (self-evident) meaning, and in the context of a sequence of such self-contained facts, the links between one fact and another are deemed equally obvious (or, alternatively, equally inconsequential). These classifications of units of thought admittedly derive from considerations not only of form and rhetoric, but also of logic and cogency. But they serve, for the moment, to allow us to distinguish among the patterns of speech we may readily identify. I have isolated nine recurrent patterns.

A. Propositions Stated Explicitly and Argued Philosophically (by appeal to probative facts)
   1. The Proposition and its Syllogistic Argument
   2. The Proposition Based on the Classification of Probative Facts
   3. The Proposition Based on the Recurrent Opinions of Sages
   4. The Narrative and its Illustrated Proposition: Parable
   5. Narrative and its Illustrated Proposition: Scriptural Story

B. Propositions Stated Implicitly but Argued Philosophically (as above)
   6. The (Implicit) Proposition Based on Facts Derived from Exegesis
   7. The Priority of Exegesis and the Limitations of Logic

C. Facts That Do Not Yield Propositions Beyond Themselves
 8. Exegetical Form with No Implicit Proposition
D. Facts That Do Not Yield Propositions Particular to the Case at Hand
 9. Dialectical Exegesis with No Implicit Proposition Pertinent to the Case at Hand but with Bearing on Large-Scale Structural Issues.

Let us now consider each of these rhetorical patterns of syntax and structure characteristic of classics of Judaism.

*1. The Proposition and its Syllogistic Argument*

The form, which is complex in its formal development, requiring (in this instance) three verses and a variety of rhetorical questions, is repeated and readily discerned. Once the point is made, there can be no developing a propositional composition that sticks to its pure form. That rigid formal convention is readily described. A verse is cited, and then a question addressed to that verse, followed by an answer, which bears in its wake secondary expansion. The whole composition in each case in the composite rests upon the intersection of two verses, a base-verse, and then a secondary verse which challenges the superficial allegation of the base-verse. This yields an "it teaches that," followed by yet a third verse, this one proving the proposed proposition. A mark of the syllogistic form is that two or more verses will be served, and the proposition by definition will concern more than the base-verse at hand. Indeed, the form cannot serve a single verse or rely for evidence on only one verse, assuredly not the base-verse.

*2. Exegetical Form with an Implicit Proposition*

This form is amazingly simple: citation of a clause of a verse followed by a sentence, generally a simple declarative one, that states a point about that clause. That form may be endlessly repeated, but it will not vastly expand in its formal traits. But a sequence of such patterns forms a complex, and that complex may be seen to demonstrate a proposition; it is the proposition, repeated throughout, that shows we have a complex, not a simple repetition, of the "commentary form." What I call "exegetical form with an implicit proposition" therefore forms a variation of other modes of setting forth and demonstrating, through probative facts, a given proposition. It follows that identifying the form in this case requires us also to define the logic of cogency that renders complex and developed in a well-crafted composite what in terms of pattern is simply a sequence of clauses or verses of a base-text followed by phrases or sentences offered in amplification in one way or another. Distinguishing rhetoric from logic is not only impossible; it misleads.

We know that we have this form because we can determine with the naked eye the implicit proposition, which will be repeated in numerous examples and so marked. A mark of exegetical form – self-evidently – is that it [1] confronts only a single passage, not being susceptible to generalization and expansion to apply to a variety of verses; and [2] does not proceed to very complicated formal expansion. Exegetical form then may serve to state and prove a proposition, e.g., a point made two or more times in succession, each time in amplification of a cited clause or verse. Exegetical form may serve a separate purpose, which is to state a fact that is self-contained and does not lead beyond itself, e.g., to a general proposition affecting two or more cases.

*3. Composite of Sayings of Sages on a Single Proposition*

This will be made up of sayings, X says, or said X, followed by diverse ways of saying the same thing or of developing the same point. What joins the whole are [1] shared theme focused upon [2] a single proposition, resting on the authority of not Scripture but [3] named sages. In logical cogency this is a counterpart to the foregoing, in that a number of sayings on a single theme – parallel to the single clause or verse above – make essentially the same point but in different ways.

Let me spell this point out. The form that involves an attributive (X says...) plus a statement of a given fact, one after another, is not terribly different, except in details of the arrangements of components of the composite, from the exegetical form that generates a proposition. That is, instead of sequences of clauses of a verse or verses, we have sequences of sages' sayings. But the proposition that is attached to the sequential clauses of a verse, or the proposition that is attached to the attributive (X says...) in either case forms part of a chain of propositions that say the same thing and so prove the same point. Once more the consideration of the logic of cogency intervenes. Just as we may have sequences of clauses of a verse followed by amplifications, in which each entry constitutes a fact unrelated to other facts fore and aft, so we may have sequences of *X says + statement*, in which no component relates to anything fore or aft. But, in point of fact, our document contains many of the former and none of the latter. The two are logically identical, but formally quite unrelated.

*4. The Particular Proposition and the Generalizing Parable*

We commence with a proposition particular to a given verse. Then we issue a fairly general comment, though that comment retains relevance solely to the case before us. What serves to turn the case into a proposition is the parable, which generalizes by comparing the case to a more general situation. Now we can see, in the concrete and the specific, a far more encompassing condition, and we can draw from the case at hand a governing rule. That is the power of the parable in the case at hand. The formal requirement is not difficult to discern.

*5. The Catalogue of Facts that Yields a Proposition*

Here we have a list of parallel items, which all together point to a simple conclusion; the conclusion may or may not be given at the end of the catalogue, but the catalogue – by definition – is pointed and follows a tight form. The catalogue's items ordinarily will be in the same syntactic form, e.g., whole sentences, balanced clauses, a set of simple nouns (as in the first instance before us). That this form finds its counterpart in sequences of names of authorities followed by statements of fact, all of them pointing toward a single proposition, or in sequences of clauses of a verse, followed by amplifications or imputations of meaning, all of them pointing toward a single, prevailing proposition, is self-evident. All three distinct forms fall into the same classification as to logic of cogency.

*6. Exegetical Form with No Implicit Proposition*

The discrete exegetical form, involving a clause of a verse or a whole verse, followed by a phrase or a sentence that imputes to the cited formula a given meaning, never stands all by itself. Very frequently, we will find a sequence of such episodic and ad hoc units of thought – simple sentences, when seen naked. But these sentences, which constitute facts, in the mind of the compositors of our document follow, in sequence if not in connection of thought, from one to the next. We know it because the compositors have made up some proportion of the whole of such episodic, naked units of thought: sentences that are simple facts. In terms of the analogy given just now, we find in the mass before us atoms that form molecules, but also atoms that do not form molecules (though no protons, no negative charges, no positive charges, all by themselves, to allow the metaphor to peter out).

*7. The Priority of Exegesis and the Limitations of Logic*

The form is a striking and blatant one:

1. Verse and its exegesis
2. Is that conclusion not a matter of logic? + logical argument
3. Refutation of the logical argument (may be protracted)
4. Repetition of verse and its exegesis

The implicit proposition before us is that exegesis, not (mere) reason, is required to yield reliable knowledge. The explicit proposition is particular to the case at hand. For our topical catalogue, the implicit proposition is important. But it is too general to shed light on any other, particular case, or to join one case to another and so to show that in many things there is one thing. But the topic and the proposition follow a highly patterned rhetorical program, and it is one that requires its own category.

*8. Dialectical Exegesis with No Implicit Proposition*

This is formally a rather complex construction, with its dialectical movement from proposition to its opposite. We start with a question addressed to the base-verse. Then "might we suppose" yields an exegesis, which answers question one. That is followed by, "I know only..., how about...?" and that yields a further exegesis, and so on down. On that basis we have to regard it as a formally distinct item, for we have not only a simple exegesis, but a secondary expansion. I see no proposition that transcends the limits of the case. Accordingly, the form is a stunning one, but in logic the matter is a set of rather simple facts, pertaining to a single case and illustrating no proposition that transcends the facts.

*9. Narrative and its Illustrated Proposition: Scriptural Story*

In a narrative on a scriptural theme, a story dramatizes a message, e.g., from Moses. The purpose of the narrative is simply to set the stage for the proposition. There is no beginning, middle, or end, and no tension and resolution. Rather we have a narrative form for containing a proposition or a lesson.

This catalogue, therefore, is misleading in one important respect. The first five forms make no provision for a completed unit of thought, all the more so a sequence of composite units of thought forming a patterned whole, that lack a clearcut proposition beyond the simple statement of fact. But a fair proportion of some entire documents is made up of highly formalized units of thought providing an amplification of a clause or a whole verse, which formalized units of thought conform to a pattern – clause, sentence with (implied) subject, verb, complement. These units of thought formally are not distinguishable, in their smallest whole examples, from exegetical units that in the aggregate contain or demonstrate an implicit proposition.

It is when we turn to the logic of cogency that we distinguish one form from the other, the non-propositional from the propositional. There is only one form for the non-propositional unit of thought, one consisting of a single thought, sentence, fact, unrelated to any other, and that is the form before us. But there are numerous well-defined syntactic patterns into which the single thought, sentence, or fact, framed as clause of a verse + phrase of amplification, are developed. So the former type of exegetical form differs, in the aggregate, from all other types of exegetical forms because by themselves they contain no proposition beyond their assertion of a set of facts – e. g., the meaning of a word or a phrase – and – and this is critical – seen in the aggregate, all together do not form a cogent whole. The non-propositional exegetical form always is an atom. The propositional exegetical form always participates in the formation of a molecule. That difference seems to me not trivial but purely formal and therefore pertinent here, not only in our analysis of the logics of the document.

From the viewpoint of form analysis, at the level of the atom, therefore, that result does not permit us to distinguish between two forms of exegesis, since the formal patterning of language is the same. From the viewpoint of modes of intelligible discourse, the distinction between the one and the other is critical. At the level of the molecule, of course, the differences are sharp and clearly marked throughout. On that basis I offer as a rhetorical, not merely logical, point of differentiation the two kinds of exegetical form, similar though they are in their smallest unit: the discrete and the composite, which, in terms of logic, also are differentiated as non-propositional and merely factual, on the one side, and propositional and highly argumentative, on the other.

A highly restricted repertoire of formal possibilities confronted the writers of materials now collected in – to revert to our favorite case – Sifré to Deuteronomy. They chose some and neglected others; a long list of formal possibilities not utilized here but extensively employed in other documents could easily emerge from large-scale comparisons of the forms of diverse writings of the canon of the Judaism of the Dual Torah. Moreover, I cannot claim to have exhausted the form-analytical program of this one document. By focusing upon the gross and blatant traits of formalization, examining a rough-and-ready mixture of rhetorical and logical traits, I have specified what I believe at the level of large-scale composition and formation of sustained units of thought, beyond the level of discrete sentences, the specific options were. And this specification yields the simple proposition that proper translating makes possible form analysis. But that means the translator has, in the course of the encounter with the original, to identify the formal traits of the writing under study.

Proper translating with close attention to the representation in formalized English of formalized Hebrew allows us to describe documents. The translation must serve to replicate the formalization and patterning of the language of the Hebrew. Then we can readily discern those forms and patterns. The reason is that the several documents exhibit important differences of rhetoric, the ordering of rhetorical patterns, and the sustained cogency of a given large-scale composition. Some documents' authorships do not take an interest in the order of rhetorical patterns; other authorships exhibit keen concern for that matter. Some documents' authorships join a large number of individual units of thought to establish a single proposition, and that sustained mode of argumentation and demonstration characterizes every single principal division of those documents. Other authorships are quite content to make one point after another, with no interest in establishing one thing out of many things.

These differences entirely suffice to show us that people made choices and carried them out. They did one thing, not another. They made decisions in the formation of the units of thought in accord with a fixed rhetorical pattern. They worked out a rhetorical program in the ordering of units of thought in accord with the diverse rhetorical patterns. They followed a distinctive policy in the composing, within a single composite, of a carefully framed proposition to be established by these ordered patterns of a limited sort. Some people did things that way, other people did things in a different way. So the differences are systematic and point to choice. It follows that the rhetorical choices of a given document are not haphazard but deliberate and point toward the presence of an authorship, that is, a plan. Translating in the proper manner allows us access to these choices.

## II. TRANSLATION AND THE REPRESENTATION OF LOGIC

By "logic" I mean something very specific and particular, and before I can set forth the relationship between translation and analysis of logical conventions of a piece of writing, I have to give a clear account of precisely what I think is subject to study. When people wish to communicate their ideas, they propose propositions for others' attention. To be understood by others, the one who frames ideas has to compose thought in ways that others understand. That understanding requires a shared conception of the connections between one thing and another, one fact and another. When we know and can describe the character of those connections – which can be quite diverse – we point to the logics of intelligible discourse for a given group, whether an entire culture or only two people who form a social entity of some sort – in our case, for an authorship. For that authorship presents statements, whether or not aimed at constituting propositions, to reach others and make sense to them – and that by definition. Such intelligible expression must evoke a shared logic so that others make the same connections that, to the authorship, prove self-evident. It is that repertoire of logics that makes the thought of one person, our authorship, intelligible to some other person(s).

In concrete terms, what this means is simple. One sentence – in modes of intelligible discourse familiar to us – not only stands beside, but generates another; a consequent statement follows from a prior one. We share a sense of connection, pertinence, relevance – the aptness of joining thought A to thought B to produce proposition One. These (only by way of example) form intelligible discourses, turning facts into statements of meaning and consequence. To conduct intelligible discourse, therefore, people make two or more statements which, in the world in which they say their piece, are deemed self-evidently to hang together and form a proposition understood by someone else in that same world. It is the matter of self-evident cogency and intelligibility, in the document at hand, that now gains our attention.

Discourse shared by others begins when one sentence joins to a second one in framing a statement (whether or not presenting a proposition) in such a way that others understand *the connection* between the two sentences. It must follow that if we are to investigate logic(s), we have to have a clear picture of where one thought begins and another ends. At that point of intersection, we can then ask, what joins this to that? Why does a framer of a document place these two completed thoughts in relationship to one another? Identifying the paragraphs allows us to ask these questions; not knowing that things relate in one way, rather than in some other, we do not know to ask them. Let me now list the four logics – modes of establishing cogency within sizable units of a document – that operate.

In the canon of Judaism as that canon had taken shape by the end of late antiquity, I see four different logics by which two sentences are deemed to cohere and to constitute a statement of consequence and intelligibility. The first of the two appeal to familiar, philosophical logic, e.g., syllogistic or propositional thought, to link sentence to sentence and paragraph to paragraph. Philosophical discourse joins units of thought through setting forth cogent propositions that are proved on the foundation of arguments from facts and reason. To establish propositions that rest upon philosophical bases, we move from the proposal of a thesis to the composition of a list of facts that prove the thesis. This – to us entirely familiar, Western – mode of scientific expression through the classification of data that, in a simple way, we may call the science of making lists (*Listenwissenschaft*), is best exemplified by the Mishnah, but it dominates, also, in such profoundly philosophical-syllogistic documents as Leviticus Rabbah as well.

The issue at hand is one of connection, that is, not of fact but of the relationship between one fact and another, which is shown in a conclusion, different from the established facts, that we propose to draw when we set up as a sequence two or more facts and claim from that sequence to propose a proposition different than, transcending, the facts at hand. We demonstrate propositions in a variety of ways, appealing to both a repertoire of probative facts and also a set of accepted modes of argument. In this way we engage in a kind of discourse that gains its logic from what, in general, we may call philosophy: the rigorous analysis and testing of propositions against the canons of an accepted reason.

We may state and demonstrate a proposition in a second way, which resorts to narrative (subject to a taxonomy of its own) both to establish and to explain connections between naked facts. A proposition (whether or not it is stated explicitly) may be set forth and demonstrated by showing through the telling of a tale (of a variety of kinds, e.g., historical, fictional, parabolic, and the like) that a sequence of events, real or imagined, shows the ineluctable truth of a given proposition. The logic of connection demonstrated through narrative, rather than philosophy, is simply stated. It is connection attained and explained by invoking some mode of narrative in which a sequence of events, first this, then that, is understood to yield a proposition, first this, then that *because of this*. That sequence both states and establishes a proposition in a way different than the philosophical and argumentative mode of propositional discourse. Whether or not the generalization is stated in so many words rarely matters because the power of well-crafted narrative is to make unnecessary explicit drawing of the moral.

We come, third, to the one genuinely odd mode of discourse in our document, one which, in our intellectual world and culture, is unfamiliar though not unknown. This logic of cogency calls upon the fixed association of data to establish connections between otherwise unrelated sentences. For example, a commentary will link successive sentences not through the cogency of the paragraphs that those sentences comprise, since there is no such cogency. Rather, the commentary attains such cogency as it exhibits by linking successive, discrete sentences to a common text; and the sentences of that text do cohere. This logic of fixed association is commonplace in many documents of Judaism beyond late antiquity, but not paramount in the canonical writings of that formative age.

Before proceeding, let me give an illustrative case that derives from our document. Here we have a sequence of absolutely unrelated sentences, made up in each instance of a clause of a verse, followed by a phrase of amplification. Nothing links one sentence (completed thought) to the ones fore or aft. Yet the compositors have presented us with what they represent side by side with sentences that do form large compositions, that is, that are linked one to the next by connections that we can readily discern. That seems to me to indicate that our authorship conceives one mode of connecting sentences to form a counterpart to another. My example derives, predictably, from Sifré to Deuteronomy.

**XXV:I**

1. A. "What kind of place are we going to? Our kinsmen have taken the heart out of us, saying, ['We saw there a people stronger and taller than we, large cities with walls sky-high, and even Anakites']" (Dt. 1:25-28):
   B. They said to him, "Moses, our lord, had we heard these things from ordinary people, we should have never believed it.
   C. "But we have heard it from people whose sons are ours and whose daughters our ours."

**XXV:II**

1. A. "We saw there a people...taller than we:"
   B. This teaches that they were tall.
2. A. "...and greater...:"
   B. This teaches that they were numerous.

**XXV:III**

1. A. "...large cities with walls sky-high, and even Anakites:"
   B. Rabban Simeon b. Gamaliel says, "In the present passage, Scriptures speak in exaggerated language: 'Hear O Israel, you are going to pass over the Jordan this day to go in to dispossess nations greater and mightier than yourself, cities great and fortified up to heaven' (Dt. 9:1).
   C. "But when God spoke to Abraham, Scripture did not use exaggerated language: 'And I will multiply your seed as the stars of the heaven' (Gen. 26:4), 'And I will make your seed as the dust of the earth'" (Gen. 13:16).

**XXV:IV**

1. A. "...and even Anakites did we see there:"
   B. This teaches that they saw giants on top of giants, in line with this verse: "Therefore pride is as a chain about their neck" (Ps. 73:6).

**XXV:V**

1. A. "And I said to you:"
   B. He stressed to them, "It is not on my own authority that I speak to you, but it is on the authority of the Holy One that I speak to you."

**XXV:VI**

1. A. "Do not be frightened and do not be afraid of them:"
   B. On what account?
   C. "for the Lord your God is the one who goes before you."

D. He said to them, "The one who did miracles for you in Egypt and all these miracles is going to do miracles for you when you enter the land:

E. "'According to all that he did for you in Egypt before your eyes' (Dt. 1:30).

F. "If you do not believe concerning what is coming, at least believe concerning what has already taken place."

We find side by side a sequence of sentences that bear no relationship or connection at all to one another. These discrete sentences have come before us in "commentary form," for instance:

> "Clause 1:" "this means A."
> "Clause 2:" "this refers to Q."

Nothing joins A and Q. Indeed, had I used symbols out of different classifications altogether, e.g., A, a letter of an alphabet, and #, which stands for something else than a sound of an alphabet, the picture would have proved still clearer. Nothing joins A to Q or A to # except that clause 2 follows clause 1. The upshot is that no proposition links A to Q or A to # and so far as there is a connection between A and Q or A and # it is not propositional. Then is there a connection at all? I think the authorship of the document that set forth matters as they did assumes that there is such a connection. For there clearly is – at the very least – an order, that is, "clause 1" is prior to "clause 2," in the text that out of clauses 1 and 2 does form an intelligible statement, that is, two connected, not merely adjacent, sentences. The connection between two facts is not established by the confluence or intersection of propositions, whether philosophically or teleologically. The upshot of the positive is that the connection is established in ways particular to the literary culture, the textual community, before us. Associations that are deemed the absolute given of all discourse are invoked, yielding no proposition at the joint of what is nonetheless an ineluctable connection.

The third logic of cogent discourse therefore rests upon the premise that an established sequence of words joins whatever is attached to those words into a set of cogent statements, even though it does not form of those statements propositions of any kind, implicit or explicit. The established sequence of words may be made up of names always associated with one another. It may be made up of a received text, with deep meanings of its own, e.g., a verse or a clause of Scripture. It may be made up of the sequence of holy days or synagogue lections, which are assumed to be known by everyone and so to connect on their own. The fixed association of these words, whether names, whether formula such as verses of Scripture, whether lists of facts, serves to link otherwise unrelated statements to one another and to form of them all not a proposition but, nonetheless, *an entirely intelligible sequence of connected or related sentences.* Even though these negative definitions intersect and in a measure cover the same ground, each requires its own specification – but I shall ask only a mite more of the reader's indulgence.

The fourth logic is set forth in discourse in which one analytical method applies to many sentences, with the result that many discrete and diverse sentences are shown to constitute a single intellectual structure. I call it the logic of cogency attained through methodical analysis. Methodologically coherent analysis imposes upon a variety of data a cogent structure that is external to all of the data, yet that imposes connection between and among facts or sentences, a connection consisting in the order and balance and meaning of them all, seen in the aggregate. One of the most common modes of intelligible discourse is to ask the same question to many things and to produce a single result, wherever that question is asked: methodical analysis of many things showing pattern and therefore order where, on the surface, none exists. In this way a variety of explanations and amplifications, topically and propositionally unrelated will be joined, a very common practice in our document. Here we have a fixed way of connecting diverse things, so showing that many things really conform to a single pattern or structure. It is the promiscuous application to a range of discrete facts of a single mode of thought, that is, a cogent analytical method.

In concrete terms, what we do through this logic, to give one example, is investigate the logical standing of details, asking whether they are meant to be restrictive or augmentative and expansive. Scripture refers to one detail, in its formulation of cases. Does the detail limit the rule to itself? Or does the detail typify, by its traits, the range to which the rule applies? Must we deal with money in the form of silver, or does silver stand for money in general? That is, do we form the rule, out of the case, restrictively or augmentatively and expansively? In answering that question once, we state a mere fact. In repeatedly asking and answering that question, we conduct a methodical analysis. And the upshot of that analysis, throughout, is to turn the details of Scripture's statement of a case into a general rule, applicable beyond the case. Overall, we show that many things form one thing, that is to say, diverse cases conform to a single logic and constitute, all together and in the aggregate, a single, highly cogent and coherent statement, even though each of the individual sentences of that statement bears slight relationship to any other of those sentences. What is important then is not the item by itself – the unit of thought seen all alone – but the repeated effect of imposing upon diverse units of thought a single analytical, that is, logical program.

Methodical analysis in fact imposes stunning cogency on otherwise unrelated facts or sentences, showing one thing out of many things. For unity of thought and discourse derives not only from what is said, or even from a set of fixed associations. It may be imposed – as our two cases have shown us – by addressing a set of fixed questions, imposing a sequence of stable procedures, to a vast variety of data. That will yield not a proposition, nor even a sequence of facts formerly unconnected but now connected, but a different mode of cogency, one that derives from showing that many things follow a single rule or may be interpreted in a single way. It is the intelligible proposition that is general and not particular, that imposes upon the whole a sense of understanding and comprehension, even though the parts of the whole do not join together. What happens, in this mode of discourse, is that we turn the particular into the general, the case into a rule, and if I had to point to one purpose of the authorship of Sifré to Deuteronomy overall, it is to turn the cases of the book of Deuteronomy into rules that conform, overall, to the way in which the Mishnah presents its rules: logically, topically, a set of philosophically defensible generalizations.

How does our mode of translation make possible the analysis of the document's logic? Here is the case with Sifré to Deuteronomy and how my reference and paragraphing system allows me to ask, and answer, the question of how distinct sentences gain cogency:

**CCCXXVI:II**

1. A. "...when he sees that their might is gone, and neither bond nor free is left:"
   B. When he sees their destruction, on account of the captivity.
   C. For all of them went off.
2. A. Another teaching concerning the phrase, "...when he sees:"
   B. When they despaired of redemption.
3. A. Another teaching concerning the phrase, "...when he sees that their might is gone, and neither bond nor free is left:"
   B. When he sees that the last penny is gone from the purse,
   C. in line with this verse: "And when they have made an end of breaking in pieces the power of the holy people, all these things shall be finished" (Dan. 12:7) [Hammer's translation].
4. A. Another teaching concerning the phrase, "...when he sees that their might is gone, and neither bond nor free is left:"
   B. When he sees that among them are no men who seek mercy for them as Moses had,
   C. in line with this verse: "Therefore he said that he would destroy them, had not Moses his chosen one stood before him in the breach" (Ps. 106:23).

5. A. Another teaching concerning the phrase, "...when he sees that their might is gone, and neither bond nor free is left:"
   B. When he sees that among them are no men who seek mercy for them as Aaron had,
   C. in line with this verse: "And he stood between the dead and the living and the plague was stayed" (Num. 17:13).
6. A. Another teaching concerning the phrase, "...when he sees that their might is gone, and neither bond nor free is left:"
   B. When he sees that there are no men who seek mercy for them as Phineas had,
   C. in line with this verse: "Then stood up Phineas and wrought judgment and so the plague was stayed" (Ps. 106:30).
7. A. Another teaching concerning the phrase, "...when he sees that their might is gone, and neither bond nor free is left:"
   B. None shut up, none [Hammer:] at large, none helping Israel.

Here is a case in which, when we see the sentences one by one, we also can identify what holds them together. It is propositional logic of a very simple kind. No. 1 introduces the basic theme invited by the base-verse, namely, Israel's disheartening condition. Then the rest of the items point to the unfortunate circumstance of Israel and the absence of effective leadership to change matters. While philosophers in the Greco-Roman tradition will have made their points concerning other topics entirely, modes of proof will surely have proved congruent to the systematic massing of probative facts, all of them pertinent, all of them appropriate to the argument and the issue.

Here is a case of the logic of fixed association, as my translation makes that logic transparent:

**CLXXVIII:III**

1. A. "...the prophet has uttered it presumptuously:"
   B. One is liable for acting presumptuously, and one is not liable for acting in error.
2. A. "...do not stand in dread of him:"
   B. Do not hesitate to hold him guilty as charged.

If we did not number and letter the items, we should have no way of asking how they relate. But as is, each numbered unit forms a single declarative sentence. No. 1 makes a distinction important only in legal theory, and No. 2 simply exhorts people to enforce the law. Nothing joins No. 1 to No. 2 except that both rest upon clauses of the same verse. The compositor of the passage took for granted that that fixed association validated his joining No. 1 to No. 2. Within distinguishing one item from the other, I should never have had reason to ask myself how they relate and what sort of logic of cogent discourse links them. Analytical translation forms the beginning of the matter.

## III. Translation as an Instrument of Analysis

My insistence upon providing a reference system within a translation, my advocacy of a translation that affords ample differentiation of the bits and pieces of thought – these aim at solving substantive and not merely formal problems. The stakes in doing so are high. My translations aim at opening doors to documents, their structure and system, not merely affording access to their contents. The premise of my work, therefore, is that a piece of writing exhibits distinctive traits, so that, as a matter of fact, we can define a document on its own, not merely as part of "the Torah" (in theological terms) or as a medium for the preservation of philological data (in scholarly ones). But do documents exhibit rhetorical and logical traits that can be conveyed in accessible form (whether in English, Modern Hebrew, or Middle [rabbinic] Hebrew)? The claim that they do follow forms that we can identify and isolate, and that they do appeal to a logic that we can define and the presence of which we demonstrate – that has now to be made to stick. And the evidence must be wholly inductive in approach and inherent in venue.

The way we translate will allow us to examine that evidence, but only on certain rigidly met conditions. We must translate a given formation of language – syntax, morphology, structure – in a single and uniform way. That will permit us to identify the formal traits of writing as these recur many times. Further, we must translate so that the smallest whole units of intelligible thought are distinguished from one another (one sentence from another, for instance). That will allow us to ask how one thought coheres with the next so as to form intelligible intellection. Again, we must translate so that completed propositions – in common parlance, paragraphs, for instance – are distinguished from other such expositions of cogent thought. When we know where a major proposition has been fully exposed, we can also ask about its relationship to other such propositions and their exposures, fore and aft. In this way we can see how large compositions are put together, e.g., propositionally or in terms of some other conception of linkage besides the one we find familiar. Translations can do all this.

By marking the units from large to small (and small to large), we can identify the pieces of evidence on which we are working; otherwise we cannot. If we can say to ourselves, "This is a complete unit of thought, a sentence," we can then compare that unit of thought to others. In this way we determine whether or not sentences conform to a single pattern. If we can show that three or five sentences follow a single, fixed pattern, e.g., in their formation and layout, then we can ask whether that same pattern recurs many times. That permits us to know whether a document appeals to a limited repertoire of formal configurations of thought (terms I shall define more adequately in due course). And, further, if we see two or more well-composed paragraphs that are set contiguous with one another, we are able to ask ourselves whether these paragraphs form part of a continuous argument, or whether each stands in splendid isolation from all others.

All of these kinds of questions concerning rhetorical and logical conventions of a document can be addressed with the right paragraphing and the right marking of those paragraphs. But without the right paragraphing and a suitable reference system – if not mine, then some other that differentiates types of units of thought by the very character used in the system itself – we can discern nothing.

Larger questions of introduction – that is, the systematic description of a text – follow in sequence, once the simple facts of the document are established. Questions I propose on the basis of inductive inquiry to answer are, for one example, is a piece of writing an episodic and ad hoc composite or is it a cogent composition? Cogency may derive from recurrent formal constructions and from tightly linked and cogent propositional arguments, set forth in proper sequence. Is it a sustained, unitary text, or a collection of discrete fragments that someone has thrown together for reasons we cannot imagine? The presence of rhetorical rules and logical protocols will suggest the former possibility, their absence, the latter.

But without analysis no one can ask these questions, and, as a matter of fact, before me, with regard to the rabbinical classics, none ever did ask that question. Yet if we do not know the answers, – if we cannot define the forms and logics of a piece of writing and compare the results to those of some other piece of writing – we cannot say whether the document makes a statement at all, or whether it simply preserves this and that about whatever. We do not know how to classify the writing even in its fundamental aspect of cogency. The very labor of translation then is the work of preparing a text for the kind of analysis these questions demand. It is the equivalent of the cell biologist's preparation of his slides. The great achievements in biology rest to begin with on the proper preparation of specimens.[2] The work seems routine. But God lives in the details.

---

[2]Reading the more accessible papers of my colleague, Professor Kenneth Miller, Biology and Medicine at Brown University has taught me that simple fact. The preparation of specimens for the various fields of biology, e.g., protein crystallography, molecular biology, and biochemistry, forms the counterpart to the act of translation here. It seems to me that no study of a document can begin without a complete retranslation of that document, and

So to conclude with the point I made in the opening lines of the preface: I have nearly completed my work of retranslating the entire canon. I did that work because I found it necessary to do so. All sustained and systematic work of description and analysis, therefore also of interpretation, depends upon the correct theory and practice of translation. For translation produces the data and forces us to identify what, within a text, we think worth noticing – to begin with, after all, for translation. That is why no serious inquiry into the classics of Judaism can start without a systematic retranslation of those classics, time and again, for age succeeding age: all learning begins in the naked encounter with the unadorned document, word by word, sentence by sentence, paragraph by paragraph, chapter by chapter, document by document: all of it, all together, but, alas, step by step. After twenty years of work of a sustained and systematic order, I am still crawling.

---

the rather episodic and ad hoc work that has been done in the introduction of documents attests to the costs exacted from those who have not begun with a complete rereading and retranslation.

# Appendix

### Hammer's Introduction to Sifré to Deuteronomy

In the following pages I reproduce a sizable selection of Reuben Hammer's Introduction to his *Sifre: A Tannaitic Commentary on the Book of Deuteronomy* (New Haven and London, 1986: Yale University Press), pp. 1-21. In this way I mean to give a full and fair hearing to another approach to introducing a rabbinic classic, quite different from my own. This introduction is meant by Hammer to serve for Sifré to Deuteronomy, not only his translation, which is given its own introduction. Hence what follows is a fair representation of how another translator has chosen to represent the same document that I have translated and introduced; in this way readers will see the choices each of us has made and evaluate the merits of the approach of both of us to the problem of introducing a classic text of Judaism. I have not reproduced all of Hammer's introduction, but I have made clear the outline and main points and given samples of the discussion of each of these points. I have, however, omitted his footnotes; the reader is asked to stipulate that these are accurate and suitable for the task. At the end of a complete section of his introduction, I mark the pages that are reproduced.

### Introduction

#### 1. Sifre on Deuteronomy (Sifre D.) as Part of the Genre of Tannaitic Midrash

Sifre D. is one of a small group of books of classical interpretation of Scripture stemming from the formative period of normative Judaism in the first centuries of the Common Era. During that time the understanding of Scripture which had continuously developed since the time of Ezra was formulated and organized, each generation adding to the work of the former generations, to create an interpretation which reflected the various opinions of the Sages, known as Tannaim, concerning the meaning of Scripture.

The term *Midrash* derives from the root *drš* which is frequently found in the Bible, referring to inquiring or seeking out the word of God, usually through a prophet. In Tannaitic literature it came to signify seeking the meaning of a Scriptural verse, in a sense seeking the word of God through the interpretation of Scripture, the received written word. Since the basic constitution, the Torah, had been established and accepted, there was no place for seeking God's will through additional personal revelation. In the Book of Ezra (7:10) *drš* is used in the sense of interpreting a text, but even earlier it meant to check or investigate what had been written. Midrash, then, means enquiry in the sense of investigating the true meaning of a text. The early Scribes were both strict guardians of the Sacred Text and conveyors of its meaning. Eventually the term came to mean that learning which is text-connected as opposed to laws which are stated without any such connection and are termed *halaḵah* or *mishnah*.

Throughout the centuries material had accumulated from the early explanations of the Scribes, from the laws enacted by the Sages, and from the legal interpretations made by the use of "a complicated system of interpretation" expanded by the various generations of teachers. This material was organized and edited by the two great schools of the second century, the School of R. ʻAḳiba and the School of R. Ishmael, into the various collections which, in a form augmented during the following century, have come down to us as Tannaitic Midrash.

It is likely that the works which we now have on hand are only part of the deliberations which actually took place. Aside from Sifre D., those extant are Meḵilta de-R. Ishmael to Exodus and Sifre on Numbers, from the School of R. Ishmael, and Sifre (or Torat Kohanim) to Leviticus from the School of R. ʻAḳiba. In addition we now have reconstructions of two more works from R. ʻAḳiba's School, the Meḵilta of R. Simeon ben Yoḥai to Exodus and Sifre Zuṭa to Numbers, as well as Genizah fragments of a Meḵilta to Deuteronomy, and Midrash Tannaim to Deuteronomy from the School of R. Ishmael.

Since the early days of critical Jewish scholarship the term "Midrash-halaḵah," i.e., interpretation of legal matters, has been used to describe these works, in order to differentiate them from "Midrash-aggaḏah," narrative interpretations, even the earliest of which was edited at a later period, and which are concerned with legends and lore rather than law.

In view of the nature of these works, however, the term "Midrash-halaḵah," with its implied limitation, may well have been an unfortunate choice, even a misnomer, since all of them include interpretations of narrative Biblical verses, sometimes of specific words, legends concerning Biblical persons, stories from the lives of the Sages themselves, theological concepts and parables which illuminate the ideas presented, as well as legal matters. In some areas we have almost word by word or verse by verse explanation, in others lengthier discourses which are connected to a verse but are actually complex discussions of specific topics. For Biblical verses which are legal in nature, the halaḵic implications are drawn, and discussions based on the *middoṯ* (principles of interpretation) are recorded, together with differences of opinion and copious citations from the Mishnah itself. The organization of the material differs widely from place to place. Since the essence of Midrash is the explanation of the meaning of Scripture, it is not surprising that the contents of the Midrash reflect the diversity of Scripture itself. Although it is true that we do not have a work from this period based on the Book of Genesis, which contains almost no legal material, the narrative portions of the other four Books of the Pentateuch are by no means stinted. In Sifre D., for example, the same verse by verse treatment given the legal sections of Deuteronomy is accorded also to the poetry of Deut. 32, while in the Meḵilta the Song at the Sea (Exod. 15) is accorded an interpretation as elaborate as that given the code of law in Exod. 21. In view of this, it would be preferable to speak of Tannaitic Midrashim, reflecting the period of their origin and authorship rather than their content.

In regard to the legal sections of these Tannaitic Midrashim, ever since the inception of the historical study of Judaism the question of their relationship to apodictic laws (Mishnah), laws without discussion, without explanations, without a specific connection to Biblical verses, has been debated. Which form developed first, Mishnah or Midrash? And what does this mean in regard to the antiquity of the legal sections of the Tannaitic Midrashim?

Urbach has traced the various points of view concerning the relationship of the two forms from the time of Krochmal on. Two definite schools may be seen: one which believes that independent apodictic laws came first, later to be strengthened by connecting them to Scripture by means of Midrash; and the other which maintains that Midrash, i.e., inquiry into the Biblical text to determine specific laws and applications, was the original way of study, from which laws emerged which were only later separated from their Biblical context and assumed the form of Mishnah. Rather than adopting either view, Urbach urges us to consider the differences in the circumstances of the times, which would account for both forms appearing at different periods. Thus the situation was not one of simple development from one form to another. In addition, he notes that Midrash – inquiry – originated with the early Scribes, who were keepers of the Scriptural text, while the Sages, a different group, were enacting independent laws. Only later was exegetical learning recognized as a legitimate source of law. The antiquity of a particular law cannot therefore be determined by its form, but only by an analysis of all the relevant sources; nor can the antiquity of a passage be fixed by its form alone.

It seems unlikely that each and every law that we have and which developed over the years did so as a result of Midrash, i.e., exposition of the Scriptural text. Unwritten laws have always existed and were recognized by the literature itself as laws "given to Moses at Sinai" and ascribed to the "Oral Torah," considered of equal antiquity to the written one.

At the same time it is equally obvious that any written work requires explanation, and the more important and sacred the text, the more likely it is to be interpreted. Thus we find that at the very moment when the sanctity and authority of the Torah was publicly proclaimed, the process of explanation, Midrash, took place, as described in the ceremony held after the return from the Babylonian exile, when Ezra gathered all the people before the Water Gate and read them the Teaching of Moses, *from early morning until midday...and they read...distinctly, and they gave the sense* (Neh. 8:2–8). Some laws developed independently, while others sprang from interpretation of the Scriptural text.

The collections of legal Midrash which we have in these Tannaitic Midrashim contain several layers of material, incorporating traditions from the early days as well as those of the latest Tannaim, and reflecting a final redaction completed after the formulation of the Mishnah by R. Judah the Prince (ca. 200 C.E.).

Within them may be found:

1. simple Midrashim, the original formulation of which may be quite ancient;
2. complex Midrashim utilizing hermeneutical rules which originated at the time of Hillel or later;
3. Midrashim which connected an established ruling with a Biblical text;
4. legal expositions, explaining the halaḵic meaning of a text.

Similarly, the narrative Midrash is also multi-layered and many-faceted, containing explanations of words, stories about the Biblical characters, theological expositions, parables, and stories about, and sayings of, the Rabbis.

These few books, then represent as close an approximation as we can form of an "official" Rabbinic interpretation of Scripture. These classical expositions are invaluable documents from the understanding of the Rabbinic approach to the Bible as well as the thinking and values of the Rabbis themselves.

**2. Sifre on Deuteronomy – Origin and Structure**

The Tannaitic Midrash to Deuteronomy is known as *Sifre,* which is the plural of the Aramaic *Sifra,* "writing" or "book." The plural form is used because the Midrashim on both Numbers and Deuteronomy appear together as one work, Sifre, i.e., Books concerning Numbers and Deuteronomy."

Sifre is referred to several times in the Talmud, and is also referred to by R. Sherira Gaon as the way in which, through oral transmission of Scriptural interpretation, the laws were passed on.

The work has been traditionally referred to as Sifre de-be Rab (see B. Ber 111b, 18b), either because, as Maimonides says in his introduction to his Code, it was thought to have been transmitted together with Sifre on Numbers and Sifra by Rab (R. Abba), the pupil of R. Judah the Prince, who founded the Sura academy in Babylonia in the 3rd century, or because, as Rashi comments (on B. Ḥul 66a), it was taught in the general academy of study, *Be Raḇ,* as distinguished from those Midrashim which were studied only by R. Ishmael's pupils. A parallel exists in D. Hoffmann's collection known as Midrash Tannaim, which he formed out of Genizah fragments and those sections of the Yemenite work entitled Midrash hag-Gadol to Deuteronomy which he judged to have originated in the School of R. Ishmael.

The text is divided into 357 sections, called *Pisḳa'ot,* of varying lengths, and covers a major portion of the Book of Deuteronomy, but not all of it. The legal sections receive comprehensive treatment, the opening narrative portions are treated selectively, and the concluding narrative portions are given full commentary. Interpretations are found on the following verses: I:1–30 (Dĕḇarim), 3:23–4:1, 6:4–9 (Wa-'eṯḥannan), II:10-25 ('Eḳeḇ), 11:26–16:16 (Rĕ'eh), 16:18–21:9 (Šofṭim), 21:20–25:19 (Kiṯeṣe'), 26:1–15 (Kiṯaḇo'), 31:14 (Niṣṣaḇim), 32:1–52 (Ha'ăzinu), 33:1–34:11 (Wĕ-zo'ṯ hab-Bera-ḵah).

The opening verses of the first two Torah lessons, the conclusion of the third lesson and the sections found in the recitation of the Shema', the entire legal portion, the command that Moses must die and that Joshua will replace him, and the conclusion of Deuteronomy – the poetry of chapters 32 and 33 (Ha'ăzinu) and the verses concerning the death of Moses – are expounded.

The fragmentary nature of some of the comments, in contrast with the extensive treatment of other sections of Deuteronomy, has, along with other problems, given rise to speculation concerning the origin and unity of the work.

This matter has been discussed at great length and in detail by Abraham Goldberg, who, in disagreement with the widely held opinion that Sifre D. is a composite work combining legal sections from the

School of R. 'Aḳiba with aggadic material from the School of R. Ishmael, demonstrates that the aggadic part is also from the School of R. 'Aḳiba. Teachings of R. Ishmael are quoted because it was the common practice of each school to quote the other as an alternate opinion. Goldberg's argument is based upon a careful analysis of both the terminology and the names of authorities in Pisḳas 1–30 which are overwhelmingly from the School of R. 'Aḳiba. The legal material of the first section of Sifre D., Pisḳas 31–44, connected to the recitation of the *Shema'*, is, however, that of R. Ishmael. Goldberg notes that this opening section, which is fragmentary and deals only with selected portions, unlike the rest of Sifre D., resembles in its structure the Mekilta, and he concludes that it also is of the School of R. Ishmael, and is indeed a continuation of Sifre on Numbers. The aggadic sections, however, even if transmitted in a work of R. Ishmael's School, reflect the School of R. 'Aḳiba, as do the aggadic sections of all of the Tannaitic Midrashim. Sifre D., then, may better be seen as a two-part work, the first part being basically the continuation of Sifre on Numbers, stemming from R. Ishmael's School, while the rest is directly from R. 'Aḳiba's.

Sifre D. contains many statements, especially parables, taught by R. Simeon which he transmitted together with material taught by his master R. 'Aḳiba as transmitted by his pupil R. Simeon ben Yoḥai, who lived in the Land of Israel during the early second century:

> R. Johanan said: the author of an anonymous Mishnah is R. Meir; of an anonymous Tosefta, R. Nehemiah; of an anonymous dictum in the Sifra, R. Judah; in the Sifre, R. Simeon; and all are taught according to the views of R. 'Aḳiba.
>
> B. Sanh 86a

Assuming that Sifre refers to Sifre D., we have here a complete list of those Tannaitic works which have survived from the School of R. 'Aḳiba. The legal sections of Mekilta on Exodus and Sifre on Numbers are products of the School of R. Ishmael. Although we have no assurance that the Sifre, or for that matter also the other works, are the same as those mentioned by the Talmud, it seems reasonable to assume that what we have includes those works. If collections existed of Midrash to the Biblical Books, the editors surely utilized them. What we have is later versions, edited, added to, or changed in ways we cannot know, into which even later marginal notes were incorporated.

Targum Onkelos, the Aramaic translation of the Pentateuch dating from the end of the 4th or the beginning of the 5th century, relies heavily on the Sifre in both the legal and the narrative sections.

Sifre D. is quoted extensively by most of the classical medieval Biblical commentators, especially Rashi, who uses it with great regularity.

As in the other Tannaitic Midrashim, laws found in the Mishnah are often quoted, usually introduced with the term *mik-kan 'omru,* literally "from this they said," which indicates that the verse in question supports the teaching of the Mishnah and thus vindicates the Mishnaic ruling. The quotations do not cite the entire Mishnah, but only the first few words, indicating that the reader is to fill in the rest from his own memory, much as the Midrash cites Biblical verses only in part. Thus although Sifre D. is an independent work which stands in its own right as a Rabbinic explanation and interpretation of Deuteronomy, in the final redaction, which we have, it is also concerned to support the Mishnah by citing the Scriptural basis for the Mishnaic ruling wherever possible.

Although the final redaction of the work was executed after the publication of the Mishnah, so that Mishnaic passages are quoted and connected with Biblical verses and their interpretation, there are signs that either versions were independent of the Mishnah, reflecting sources which the Mishnah itself may have used, or citing laws which differ from the Mishnah and thus represent either earlier laws later changed or different laws rejected by the Mishnah's codifier.

Sifre's view that the Shema' must be recited aloud (Piṣka 31) does not reflect the Mishnah, which says this is not necessary (Ber 2:3). This law preceded the Mishnah, as both Finkelstein and Lieberman have shown. Finkelstein has cited other cases as well which indicate that sometimes the later redaction, for whatever reason, did not change all early material to make it conform with the Mishnah. In his study of Bik 1:1, D. Halivni has shown that Sifre has used different verses from those cited in the Mishnah for the same laws, indicating that both drew upon more ancient laws and found appropriate verses. At a later stage, however, the Mishnah's wording was added to that of Sifre.

As do all other classical Rabbinic works, Sifre D. contains several literary layers. The earliest redactions are those from the Schools of R. 'Aḳiba and R. Ishmael, which form the basic matter of the work and contain material from earlier times, followed by the main portion which was that of R. 'Aḳiba's pupils. Sifre has further material from the time of R. Judah the Prince and a post-Mishnaic layer in which the latest authorities quoted are R. Judah's disciples of the third century, such as R. Benaiah. Lieberman has pointed to sections containing quotations from actual speeches used in the pagan world, and concludes that "the date of the text is not later than the beginning of the third century." It thus seems quite certain that the basic work was edited by the pupils of the pupils of R. Judah in the third century and was compiled in the Land of Israel, as was all of the Tannaitic literature, (p. 1-6).

**3. Interpretive Methods and Formulas**

The essence of Midrash, as the name itself implies, is the elucidation of the Biblical text. In the case of a legal text, this implies a discussion of the legal practices involved and the connection of the Biblical text to the accepted halaḵah as formulated in an authoritative Mishnah. This includes argumentation citing the various conclusions that one might reach and formulation of the correct interpretation. For the most part, the Tannaitic Midrashim are marked by the use of standard formulas of interpretation, including those that form part of the accepted hermeneutical rules utilized by Hillel the Elder and later elaborated and formalized into the thirteen principles of R. Ishmael. Since Sifre D. is basically from the School of R. ʻAḳiba, however, his methods are those most often encountered. While R. Ishmael approached the text by the use of highly formalized and technical methods of interpretation and did not assume that the interpretations could be based on peculiarities of language ("Scripture uses normal language"), R. ʻAḳiba used methods which included interpretation of every word, including "only" and *'eṯ,* a particle indicating the definite predicate ("words are amplifications"), as well as using the traditional reading of Scripture *(ḳĕri)* and not only the written consonantal spelling *(kĕṯiḇ).* In addition, R. ʻAḳiba used the more inclusive interpretive principle of *ribbuy u-miʻṭ,* "the general followed by the particular subsumes everything which is like the particular." These hermeneutics appear in Sifre D. as we see in the following examples...(pp. 6-7).

*Formulaic Words and Phrases*

In order to understand these interpretations, it is helpful to note the more commonly used phrases and words which appear as technical terms connecting Biblical verses and their interpretations.

*The prefix šĕ, "that," appears as an introduction to an* interpretation, in the sense of "this indicates that...." or "so that...." At times it need not be translated at all, since it may do little more than indicate that an interpretation follows...(p. 10).

*Rejection of the Simple Meaning*

One of the prominent literary characteristics of the work is the search for a deeper meaning following the rejection of the more obvious surface meaning of a Scriptural verse or tail. Sifre D. begins with an overall view of a personalty, for example, and then decides that in view of what we know about that person's entire life and work a particular recorded incident contradicts logical expectation and therefore cannot mean what it seems to mean. A different interpretation of the text is then sought and offered. For example, we read in Piṣka 9:

> *I am not able to bear you myself alone* (1:9): Is it possible that Moses could not sit in judgment over Israel, this man who had brought them out of Egypt, who had split the sea asunder for them, who had brought down the manna for them, who had fetched the quails for them, and had performed other signs and miracles for them? Such a man could not sit in judgment over them? Rather, he spoke to them thus: *The Lord your God hath multiplied you* (1:10) upon the backs of your judges.

In view of our overall knowledge of Moses, such a thing is not possible, therefore the meaning must be otherwise, since it must make sense. See Piṣka 31 for several other examples of this.

Similarly, a statement cannot be taken at face value if it contradicts other facts. The entire work, for example, begins with the question, how can we take the first verse of Deuteronomy literally, with its implication that what follows is the record of all that Moses spoke, when we know that he also said many other things? Obviously the real meaning must be something else:

> *These are the words which Moses spoke* (1:1): Did Moses prophesy nothing but these words? Did he not write the entire Torah, as it is said, *And Moses wrote this Torah* (31:9)? Why then does the verse state, *These are the words which Moses spoke?* Hence we learn that they were words of rebuke, as it is said, *But Jeshurun waxed fat, and kicked* (32:15).
>
> Piṣka 1

It is therefore taken to mean that we are dealing with harsh words alone, with rebuke.

Similarly, when Scripture says "take men" when commanding the appointment of judges, the question is asked, why did Scripture say this, seeing that no one would even think of appointing women to such a post? The words must therefore imply something else:

> *Men* (1:13): Would we ever think of appointing women? Why then does the verse say *men?* To indicate men that are as multifaceted as a mosaic, that is to say, men who are trustworthy and suitable.
>
> Piṣka 13

Many such sections begin with the phrase "Would we ever think...?" indicating a quest for the logical and consistent meaning in the face of the "impossible" surface meaning – impossible either because it contradicts other facts or givens or because it is too obvious for Scripture to have even bothered to state it.

Other examples may be found in Piskas 153, 298, and 342.

*Repetition of the Interpretation*

Finally we should note that it is characteristic of Sifre D. that particular interpretive phrases are connected to a specific word or phrase and are then repeated whenever that word appears. The appropriateness of the interpretation is questionable in some cases; the comment may have been meaningful in its original place, but is either meaningless or inappropriate when repeated elsewhere. It is impossible to know whether these repetitions are ancient or reflect the work of some later editor who simply copied the explanation of a phrase whenever the phrase recurred. Being cognizant of the latter possibility, however, helps one to avoid a great deal of needless interpretation and search after some deeper intent on the part of the interpreter when none may have existed. See, for example, the case of the clause *So shalt thou put away the evil from the midst of thee* (Deut. 13:6), which, whenever it occurs in Sifre D., is followed by the comment "remove the evildoer from Israel" (Piska 86, 151, 155, 186, 240, etc.).

**4. Basic Homiletic Themes and Ideas**

R. Simlai remarked that the Torah begins and ends with acts of loving-kindness (B. Soṭa 14a). One might say that Sifre D. begins with rebuke and ends with reconciliation. The Book of Deuteronomy itself is a similar mixture, with its significant stretches of denunciation and predictions of dire punishment tempered with words of comfort and Moses' blessing his people.

Deuteronomy predicts national disaster but also national revival and ultimate triumph. It was written before the exile, possibly in the hope of preventing it by urging fidelity to God's word which would bring His favor. Sifre D., on the other hand, came into being hundreds of years later, when there had been not one but two destructions of the nation and of the Temple, when the political structure and independence of the nation had been dissolved and the challenges to the legitimacy of Judaism were at their height. It was important, therefore, to strengthen the authority of Rabbinic law and to demonstrate the divine nature of Scripture by interpreting the legal portions of Deuteronomy in such a way as to integrate the halakah with Scriptural verses and highlight the relevance of each verse, indeed each word, of the Bible. By the time of the final editing of the Sifre in the third century C.E. the problem was not how to avert disaster by inculcating obedience, threatening punishment, or promising reward, but how to sustain Jewish life through hope for the future by reaffirmation of the basis of Judaism: the eternal relationship between God and Israel.

Thus, although Sifre begins with a famous section which goes even further than Deuteronomy itself in chastising the people for their sins from the time of the Exodus onward and in emphasizing the fact that this is a work of rebuke, other sections tend to soften the punishment and accentuate the eventual comfort and restoration. This may be illustrated by the following passage, which appears toward the end of the work:

> *Happy art thou, O Israel, who is like unto thee?* (33:29): Israel says, *Who is like unto thee, O Lord, among the mighty?* (Exod. 15:11), and the holy spirit responds *Happy art thou, O Israel. Happy art thou, O Israel:* All Israel gathered together before Moses and said to him, "Our master Moses, tell us what good things the Holy One, blessed be He, has in store for use in the future." He replied, "I do not know what to tell you. Happy are you with that which is prepared for you."
>
> Piska 356

Although it is undoubtedly true that the argument from silence is no argument, one may wonder whether the fact that the harsh passages in Deut. 27 and 28 – the curses – which are so crucial to the Biblical text, do not receive any Midrashic attention in Sifre D., is totally accidental...(pp. 14–17).

Prominent in Sifre D. are the following themes:

1. The importance of the people of Israel. Although the sections on rebuke are replete with condemnation of Israel, which must be seen not only as a reflection of historical events but also as a comment on current affairs (see Piskas 12, 14, 20, 24, and numerous sections in Ha'ăzinu), Sifre misses no opportunity to praise the people and to stress God's positive relationship to them, emphasizing the unbroken nature of this relationship. To reassure the Jewish people in the hour of tragedy and depression and to refute those who held otherwise, the Sages and editors of Sifre stress that Israel is the favored of God (Piska 15), that love and intimacy remain intact between God and Israel (Piskas 355, 356). God is indeed the Master of the universe, but His relationship with Israel is special and unique (Piska 31). Regardless of what they may have misdone, God forgives His people (Piska 30) and feels no hatred toward them (Piska 24).

2. If Israel is beloved and will be redeemed, the nations who have dealt cruelly with her are condemned and will suffer the consequences of their cruelty. Reflecting the bitterness of the post-destruction era,

Sifre, especially in its latter sections, describes the nations in harsh terms and sees them as doomed to repeated destruction.

3. Closely allied to the preceding themes is Sifre's attitude toward Jacob, the prototype of Israel, and his children. The theme of Jacob's special merit and of the superiority of his entire family appears in several places in the work, such as Piṣka 312, and is dwelt upon at great length in the complex composition found in Piṣka 31. As has been discussed in detail by E. Mihaly, this may be a response to Christian claims and certainly strengthens Israel's claim to the position of the exclusive people of the covenant. Only those who are descended from Jacob can claim to be part of this relationship, for the others who sprang from Abraham or Isaac are mere refuse. Only conversion to Judaism will bring one not descended from Jacob into this special relationship (Piṣka 354). In this connection one should also note the heavily critical attitude toward the nations of the world, including a different attitude toward the seven Noachide commandments than that usually taken (see B. Sanh 56a; it is echoed in a similar aggadic section, B. AZ, beginning). These laws were not observed by the other nations, and were therefore taken from them and given as additional commandments to Israel.

4. In contrast to Jacob, Abraham appears in quite a different capacity. He brings about a revolutionary change in the world and in God's relationship to it, but it is in his role as an individual that he does this, and the covenant relationship is not emphasized.

Abraham's major merit is seen in the fact that he brought knowledge of God into the world (Piṣka 354). It was Abraham who changed God's relationship to the world, moving Him from emphasis upon justice (or even severity) to mercy through the sufferings of love imposed upon Abraham which continued upon the Israelites (Piṣka 311). The Christian claim that redemptive suffering came first and exclusively through Jesus is countered here by the Jewish claim that it had existed before and has always been the role of the people of Israel.

In addition to the places where Abraham and Jacob are compared in respect to the merits of their progeny, they are also compared once (Piṣka 336) in respect to their observance of God's commands. Here, too, the emphasis is upon Jacob, for Abraham is said to have observed only one command, whereas Jacob is anachronistically credited with observing the entire Torah!

5. The personality of Moses is dealt with extensively, as was to be expected, since Deuteronomy is couched in the form of a speech given by Moses, and his plea to let him enter Israel and the story of his death are also contained in this book. Sifre D. describes his unhappiness with the conduct of the people (Piṣkas 1–2) and their attitude toward him

(Piṣka 14), his concern for the people (Piṣka 342) and for the leader who is to follow him (Piṣkas 304–05). His death is depicted in a particularly artistic story which combines humor and great poignancy (Piṣka 326).

6. Just as the merit of the people of Israel is stressed, so is the merit and worth of the Land of Israel. Using the slightest of pretexts, the editors have included a highly sophisticated section on the merits of the Land. Its beauty, its fruitfulness, its uniqueness are all commented upon at great length in what can only be described as a rhapsodic paean to a land which realistically speaking was suffering a decline (Piṣkas 37–40; see also Piṣkas 316 and 354). To a people suffering destruction, economic problems, and foreign subjugation, these words served to reaffirm the Biblical promises and the centrality of the Land to Judaism.

7. Questions of God's nature and judgment of peoples and individuals are discussed. As Kadushin has shown in his studies of Rabbinic thinking and of Tannaitic texts, the two qualities of God, mercy and justice, encompass the tension in the world and the various ways in which God is experienced according to Rabbinic doctrine (see Piṣkas 49, 311, 306).

This also results in an interesting attitude toward human merit. Basing itself upon the merits of such great men as Moses and David, the text adopts a posture which became normative for Judaism in the liturgy of the High Holy Days: God's graciousness to man, who can never be truly deserving of the mercy that he is shown (Piṣka 26). Without denying the existence of human merit, we are taught that merit is never used in a plea to God, but only His graciousness, which is given *ḥinnam*, "unearned," to man.

8. On the other hand, in human relationships, justice must be the rule. The need for a good system of justice and for the seriousness with which the work of the judge should be treated is emphasized time and time again (Piṣkas 9, 17, 29).

9. The Torah and its glory is an obvious theme which is taken up in Sifre as well. It is the antidote to the evil Inclination (Piṣka 45). Methods for its study are discussed in detail (Piṣka 48). It is Israel's exclusive property (Piṣka 345).

10. An interesting point is the problem of the observance of the commandments outside of the Land (Piṣkas 25, 43). Since the problem of exile was a real one, Israel-centered Sifre went out of its way to indicate that such observance outside of the Land was no more than practice for the true observance, which can be practiced only in the Land itself.

Taken as a whole, then the aggadic sections of this work reflect the basic value scheme of Pharisaic Judaism, and take a stance intended to strengthen the Jews' resolve in the face of adversity. The historical background is that of a time of trouble, suffering, even disaster: the situation of the Jewish people in the Land of Israel during and after the Hadrianic persecution and the failure of the Bar Kokhba revolt. There are, of course, stories, legends, and interpretations which originated long before that time. Not missing either are pointed, though indirect, answers to the challenges of the newly emerging Christian group.

In spite of all this Sifre does not conceal the faults of the Jewish people, their rebelliousness, and their unfaithfulness. In reviewing the stern admonitions of Moses, it thus also criticizes the contemporary scene. On the other hand, it stoutly affirms the status of the people, both from the events in the lives of the Patriarchs and from Scriptural promises, as God's peculiar treasure with a unique relationship to Him. It denounces the claims of the nations or of Christianity to have displaced them. It draws a picture of the Land of Israel as the Promised Land and the land of promise, and reaffirms the Torah as the supreme object of value. The people of Israel, the Land of Israel, and the Torah of Israel are placed squarely in the center of the values to be taught.

As for God, He is the God of Israel while being also the universal God of all nations. He is God of mercy and God of righteousness, whose mercy far exceeds His justice, who expects obedience and moral conduct from Israel, but grants His favor to men out of His grace and not because of their deeds.

The work, especially in the later sections, is permeated by Messianic expectation. This is what will happen in the future – tomorrow – in the renewed world. Then Israel, His people, will be revealed and restored in all their glory. The failures and punishments of the past will be forgotten and obliterated. The nations will be seen for what they are and will be punished (pp. 17–21).

# Index

Brown Judaic Studies

| | | |
|---|---|---|
| 140001 | *Approaches to Ancient Judaism I* | William S. Green |
| 140002 | *The Traditions of Eleazar Ben Azariah* | Tzvee Zahavy |
| 140003 | *Persons and Institutions in Early Rabbinic Judaism* | William S. Green |
| 140004 | *Claude Goldsmid Montefiore on the Ancient Rabbis* | Joshua B. Stein |
| 140005 | *The Ecumenical Perspective and the Modernization of Jewish Religion* | S. Daniel Breslauer |
| 140006 | *The Sabbath-Law of Rabbi Meir* | Robert Goldenberg |
| 140007 | *Rabbi Tarfon* | Joel Gereboff |
| 140008 | *Rabban Gamaliel II* | Shamai Kanter |
| 140009 | *Approaches to Ancient Judaism II* | William S. Green |
| 140010 | *Method and Meaning in Ancient Judaism* | Jacob Neusner |
| 140011 | *Approaches to Ancient Judaism III* | William S. Green |
| 140012 | *Turning Point: Zionism and Reform Judaism* | Howard R. Greenstein |
| 140013 | *Buber on God and the Perfect Man* | Pamela Vermes |
| 140014 | *Scholastic Rabbinism* | Anthony J. Saldarini |
| 140015 | *Method and Meaning in Ancient Judaism II* | Jacob Neusner |
| 140016 | *Method and Meaning in Ancient Judaism III* | Jacob Neusner |
| 140017 | *Post Mishnaic Judaism in Transition* | Baruch M. Bokser |
| 140018 | *A History of the Mishnaic Law of Agriculture: Tractate Maaser Sheni* | Peter J. Haas |
| 140019 | *Mishnah's Theology of Tithing* | Martin S. Jaffee |
| 140020 | *The Priestly Gift in Mishnah: A Study of Tractate Terumot* | Alan. J. Peck |
| 140021 | *History of Judaism: The Next Ten Years* | Baruch M. Bokser |
| 140022 | *Ancient Synagogues* | Joseph Gutmann |
| 140023 | *Warrant for Genocide* | Norman Cohn |
| 140024 | *The Creation of the World According to Gersonides* | Jacob J. Staub |
| 140025 | *Two Treatises of Philo of Alexandria: A Commentary on De Gigantibus and Quod Deus Sit Immutabilis* | David Winston/John Dillon |
| 140026 | *A History of the Mishnaic Law of Agriculture: Kilayim* | Irving Mandelbaum |
| 140027 | *Approaches to Ancient Judaism IV* | William S. Green |
| 140028 | *Judaism in the American Humanities* | Jacob Neusner |
| 140029 | *Handbook of Synagogue Architecture* | Marilyn Chiat |
| 140030 | *The Book of Mirrors* | Daniel C. Matt |
| 140031 | *Ideas in Fiction: The Works of Hayim Hazaz* | Warren Bargad |
| 140032 | *Approaches to Ancient Judaism V* | William S. Green |
| 140033 | *Sectarian Law in the Dead Sea Scrolls: Courts, Testimony and the Penal Code* | Lawrence H. Schiffman |
| 140034 | *A History of the United Jewish Appeal: 1939-1982* | Marc L. Raphael |
| 140035 | *The Academic Study of Judaism* | Jacob Neusner |
| 140036 | *Woman Leaders in the Ancient Synagogue* | Bernadette Brooten |
| 140037 | *Formative Judaism: Religious, Historical, and Literary Studies* | Jacob Neusner |
| 140038 | *Ben Sira's View of Women: A Literary Analysis* | Warren C. Trenchard |
| 140039 | *Barukh Kurzweil and Modern Hebrew Literature* | James S. Diamond |

| | | |
|---|---|---|
| 140040 | *Israeli Childhood Stories of the Sixties: Yizhar, Aloni,Shahar, Kahana-Carmon* | Gideon Telpaz |
| 140041 | *Formative Judaism II: Religious, Historical, and Literary Studies* | Jacob Neusner |
| 140042 | *Judaism in the American Humanities II: Jewish Learning and the New Humanities* | Jacob Neusner |
| 140043 | *Support for the Poor in the Mishnaic Law of Agriculture: Tractate Peah* | Roger Brooks |
| 140044 | *The Sanctity of the Seventh Year: A Study of Mishnah Tractate Shebiit* | Louis E. Newman |
| 140045 | *Character and Context: Studies in the Fiction of Abramovitsh, Brenner, and Agnon* | Jeffrey Fleck |
| 140046 | *Formative Judaism III: Religious, Historical, and Literary Studies* | Jacob Neusner |
| 140047 | *Pharaoh's Counsellors: Job, Jethro, and Balaam in Rabbinic and Patristic Tradition* | Judith Baskin |
| 140048 | *The Scrolls and Christian Origins: Studies in the Jewish Background of the New Testament* | Matthew Black |
| 140049 | *Approaches to Modern Judaism I* | Marc Lee Raphael |
| 140050 | *Mysterious Encounters at Mamre and Jabbok* | William T. Miller |
| 140051 | *The Mishnah Before 70* | Jacob Neusner |
| 140052 | *Sparda by the Bitter Sea: Imperial Interaction in Western Anatolia* | Jack Martin Balcer |
| 140053 | *Hermann Cohen: The Challenge of a Religion of Reason* | William Kluback |
| 140054 | *Approaches to Judaism in Medieval Times I* | David R. Blumenthal |
| 140055 | *In the Margins of the Yerushalmi: Glosses on the English Translation* | Jacob Neusner |
| 140056 | *Approaches to Modern Judaism II* | Marc Lee Raphael |
| 140057 | *Approaches to Judaism in Medieval Times II* | David R. Blumenthal |
| 140058 | *Midrash as Literature: The Primacy of Documentary Discourse* | JacobNeusner |
| 140059 | *The Commerce of the Sacred: Mediation of the Divine Among Jews in the Graeco-Roman Diaspora* | Jack N. Lightstone |
| 140060 | *Major Trends in Formative Judaism I: Society and Symbol in Political Crisis* | Jacob Neusner |
| 140061 | *Major Trends in Formative Judaism II: Texts, Contents, and Contexts* | Jacob Neusner |
| 140062 | *A History of the Jews in Babylonia I: The Parthian Period* | Jacob Neusner |
| 140063 | *The Talmud of Babylonia: An American Translation. XXXII: Tractate Arakhin* | Jacob Neusner |
| 140064 | *Ancient Judaism: Debates and Disputes* | Jacob Neusner |
| 140065 | *Prayers Alleged to Be Jewish: An Examination of the Constitutiones Apostolorum* | David Fiensy |
| 140066 | *The Legal Methodology of Hai Gaon* | Tsvi Groner |
| 140067 | *From Mishnah to Scripture: The Problem of the Unattributed Saying* | Jacob Neusner |
| 140068 | *Halakhah in a Theological Dimension* | David Novak |

| | | |
|---|---|---|
| 140069 | *From Philo to Origen: Middle Platonism in Transition* | Robert M. Berchman |
| 140070 | *In Search of Talmudic Biography: The Problem of the Attributed Saying* | Jacob Neusner |
| 140071 | *The Death of the Old and the Birth of the New: The Framework of the Book of Numbers and the Pentateuch* | Dennis T. Olson |
| 140072 | *The Talmud of Babylonia: An American Translation. XVII: Tractate Sotah* | Jacob Neusner |
| 140073 | *Understanding Seeking Faith: Essays on the Case of Judaism. Volume Two: Literature, Religion and the Social Study of Judiasm* | JacobNeusner |
| 140074 | *The Talmud of Babylonia: An American Translation. VI: Tractate Sukkah* | Jacob Neusner |
| 140075 | *Fear Not Warrior: A Study of 'al tira' Pericopes in the Hebrew Scriptures* | Edgar W. Conrad |
| 140076 | *Formative Judaism IV: Religious, Historical, and Literary Studies* | Jacob Neusner |
| 140077 | *Biblical Patterns in Modern Literature* | David H. Hirsch/ Nehama Aschkenasy |
| 140078 | *The Talmud of Babylonia: An American Translation I: Tractate Berakhot* | Jacob Neusner |
| 140079 | *Mishnah's Division of Agriculture: A History and Theology of Seder Zeraim* | Alan J. Avery-Peck |
| 140080 | *From Tradition to Imitation: The Plan and Program of Pesiqta Rabbati and Pesiqta deRab Kahana* | Jacob Neusner |
| 140081 | *The Talmud of Babylonia: An American Translation. XXIIIA: Tractate Sanhedrin, Chapters 1-3* | Jacob Neusner |
| 140082 | *Jewish Presence in T. S. Eliot and Franz Kafka* | Melvin Wilk |
| 140083 | *School, Court, Public Administration: Judaism and its Institutions in Talmudic Babylonia* | Jacob Neusner |
| 140084 | *The Talmud of Babylonia: An American Translation. XXIIIB: Tractate Sanhedrin, Chapters 4-8* | Jacob Neusner |
| 140085 | *The Bavli and Its Sources: The Question of Tradition in the Case of Tractate Sukkah* | Jacob Neusner |
| 140086 | *From Description to Conviction: Essays on the History and Theology of Judaism* | Jacob Neusner |
| 140087 | *The Talmud of Babylonia: An American Translation. XXIIIC: Tractate Sanhedrin, Chapters 9-11* | Jacob Neusner |
| 140088 | *Mishnaic Law of Blessings and Prayers: Tractate Berakhot* | Tzvee Zahavy |
| 140089 | *The Peripatetic Saying: The Problem of the Thrice-Told Tale in Talmudic Literature* | Jacob Neusner |
| 140090 | *The Talmud of Babylonia: An American Translation. XXVI: Tractate Horayot* | Martin S. Jaffee |
| 140091 | *Formative Judaism V: Religious, Historical, and Literary Studies* | Jacob Neusner |
| 140092 | *Essays on Biblical Method and Translation* | Edward Greenstein |
| *140093* | *The Integrity of Leviticus Rabbah* | Jacob Neusner |
| 140094 | *Behind the Essenes: History and Ideology of the Dead Sea Scrolls* | Philip R. Davies |

| | | |
|---|---|---|
| 140095 | *Approaches to Judaism in Medieval Times, Volume III* | David R. Blumenthal |
| 140096 | *The Memorized Torah: The Mnemonic System of the Mishnah* | Jacob Neusner |
| 140098 | *Sifre to Deuteronomy: An Analytical Translation. Volume One: Pisqaot One through One Hundred Forty-Three. Debarim, Waethanan, Eqeb* | Jacob Neusner |
| 140099 | *Major Trends in Formative Judaism III: The Three Stages in the Formation of Judaism* | Jacob Neusner |
| 140101 | *Sifre to Deuteronomy: An Analytical Translation. Volume Two: Pisqaot One Hundred Forty-Four through Three Hundred Fifty-Seven. Shofetim, Ki Tese, Ki Tabo, Nesabim, Ha'azinu, Zot Habberakhah* | Jacob Neusner |
| 140102 | *Sifra: The Rabbinic Commentary on Leviticus* | Jacob Neusner/ Roger Brooks |
| 140103 | *The Human Will in Judaism* | Howard Eilberg-Schwartz |
| 140104 | *Genesis Rabbah: Volume 1. Genesis 1:1 to 8:14* | Jacob Neusner |
| 140105 | *Genesis Rabbah: Volume 2. Genesis 8:15 to 28:9* | Jacob Neusner |
| 140106 | *Genesis Rabbah: Volume 3. Genesis 28:10 to 50:26* | Jacob Neusner |
| 140107 | *First Principles of Systemic Analysis* | Jacob Neusner |
| 140108 | *Genesis and Judaism* | Jacob Neusner |
| 140109 | *The Talmud of Babylonia: An American Translation. XXXV: Tractates Meilah and Tamid* | Peter J. Haas |
| 140110 | *Studies in Islamic and Judaic Traditions* | William Brinner/Stephen Ricks |
| 140111 | *Comparative Midrash: The Plan and Program of Genesis Rabbah and Leviticus Rabbah* | Jacob Neusner |
| 140112 | *The Tosefta: Its Structure and its Sources* | Jacob Neusner |
| 140113 | *Reading and Believing* | Jacob Neusner |
| 140114 | *The Fathers According to Rabbi Nathan* | Jacob Neusner |
| 140115 | *Etymology in Early Jewish Interpretation: The Hebrew Names in Philo* | Lester L. Grabbe |
| 140116 | *Understanding Seeking Faith: Essays on the Case of Judaism. Volume One: Debates on Method, Reports of Results* | Jacob Neusner |
| 140117 | *The Talmud of Babylonia. An American Translation. VII: Tractate Besah* | Alan J. Avery-Peck |
| 140118 | *Sifre to Numbers: An American Translation and Explanation, Volume One: Sifre to Numbers 1-58* | Jacob Neusner |
| 140119 | *Sifre to Numbers: An American Translation and Explanation, Volume Two: Sifre to Numbers 59-115* | Jacob Neusner |
| 140120 | *Cohen and Troeltsch: Ethical Monotheistic Religion and Theory of Culture* | Wendell S. Dietrich |
| 140121 | *Goodenough on the History of Religion and on Judaism* | Jacob Neusner/ Ernest Frerichs |
| 140122 | *Pesiqta deRab Kahana I: Pisqaot One through Fourteen* | Jacob Neusner |
| 140123 | *Pesiqta deRab Kahana II: Pisqaot Fifteen through Twenty-Eight and Introduction to Pesiqta deRab Kahana* | Jacob Neusner |
| 140124 | *Sifre to Deuteronomy: Introduction* | Jacob Neusner |

| | | |
|---|---|---|
| 140126 | *A Conceptual Commentary on Midrash Leviticus Rabbah: Value Concepts in Jewish Thought* | Max Kadushin |
| 140127 | *The Other Judaisms of Late Antiquity* | Alan F. Segal |
| 140128 | *Josephus as a Historical Source in Patristic Literature through Eusebius* | Michael Hardwick |
| 140129 | *Judaism: The Evidence of the Mishnah* | Jacob Neusner |
| 140131 | *Philo, John and Paul: New Perspectives on Judaism and Early Christianity* | Peder Borgen |
| 140132 | *Babylonian Witchcraft Literature* | Tzvi Abusch |
| 140133 | *The Making of the Mind of Judaism: The Formative Age* | Jacob Neusner |
| 140135 | *Why No Gospels in Talmudic Judaism?* | Jacob Neusner |
| 140136 | *Torah: From Scroll to Symbol Part III: Doctrine* | Jacob Neusner |
| 140137 | *The Systemic Analysis of Judaism* | Jacob Neusner |
| 140138 | *Sifra: An Analytical Translation Vol. 1* | Jacob Neusner |
| 140139 | *Sifra: An Analytical Translation Vol. 2* | Jacob Neusner |
| 140140 | *Sifra: An Analytical Translation Vol. 3* | Jacob Neusner |
| 140141 | *Midrash in Context: Exegesis in Formative Judaism* | Jacob Neusner |
| 140143 | *Oxen, Women or Citizens? Slaves in the System of Mishnah* | Paul V. Flesher |
| 140144 | *The Book of the Pomegranate* | Elliot R. Wolfson |
| 140145 | *Wrong Ways and Right Ways in the Study of Formative Judaism* | Jacob Neusner |
| 140146 | *Sifra in Perspective: The Documentary Comparison of the Midrashim of Ancient Judaism* | Jacob Neusner |
| 140148 | *Mekhilta According to Rabbi Ishmael: An Analytical Translation Volume I* | Jacob Neusner |
| 140149 | *The Doctrine of the Divine Name: An Introduction to Classical Kabbalistic Theology* | Stephen G. Wald |
| 140150 | *Water into Wine and the Beheading of John the Baptist* | Roger Aus |
| 140151 | *The Formation of the Jewish Intellect* | Jacob Neusner |
| 140152 | *Mekhilta According to Rabbi Ishmael: An Introduction to Judaism's First Scriptural Encyclopaedia* | Jacob Neusner |
| 140153 | *Understanding Seeking Faith. Volume Three* | Jacob Neusner |
| 140154 | *Mekhilta According to Rabbi Ishmael: An Analytical Translation Volume Two* | Jacob Neusner |
| 140155 | *Goyim: Gentiles and Israelites in Mishnah-Tosefta* | Gary P. Porton |
| 140156 | *A Religion of Pots and Pans?* | Jacob Neusner |
| 140157 | *Claude Montefiore and Christianity* | Maurice Gerald Bowler |
| 140158 | *The Philosopical Mishnah Volume III* | Jacob Neusner |
| 140159 | *From Ancient Israel to Modern Judaism Volume 1: Intellect in Quest of Understanding* | Neusner/Frerichs/Sarna |
| 140160 | *The Social Study of Judaism Volume I* | Jacob Neusner |
| 140161 | *Philo's Jewish Identity* | Alan Mendelson |
| 140162 | *The Social Study of Judaism Volume II* | Jacob Neusner |
| 140163 | *The Philosophical Mishnah Volume I : The Initial Probe* | Jacob Neusner |
| 140164 | *The Philosophical Mishnah Volume II : The Tractates Agenda: From Abodah Zarah Through Moed Qatan* | Jacob Neusner |
| 140166 | *Women's Earliest Records* | Barbara S. Lesko |

| | | |
|---|---|---|
| 140167 | *The Legacy of Hermann Cohen* | William Kluback |
| 140168 | *Method and Meaning in Ancient Judaism* | Jacob Neusner |
| 140169 | *The Role of the Messenger and Message in the Ancient Near East* | John T. Greene |
| 140171 | *Abraham Heschel's Idea of Revelation* | Lawerence Perlman |
| 140172 | *The Philosophical Mishnah Volume IV: The Repertoire* | Jacob Neusner |
| 140173 | *From Ancient Israel to Modern Judaism Volume 2: Intellect in Quest of Understanding* | Neusner/Frerichs/Sarna |
| 140174 | *From Ancient Israel to Modern Judaism Volume 3: Intellect in Quest of Understanding* | Neusner/Frerichs/Sarna |
| 140175 | *From Ancient Israel to Modern Judaism Volume 4: Intellect in Quest of Understanding* | Neusner/Frerichs/Sarna |
| 140176 | *Translating the Classics of Judaism: In Theory and In Practice* | Jacob Neusner |
| 140177 | *Profiles of a Rabbi: Synoptic Opportunities in Readings About Jesus* | Bruce Chilton |
| 140178 | *Studies in Islamic and Judaic Traditions II* | William Brinner/Stephen Ricks |

Brown Studies on Jews and Their Societies

| | | |
|---|---|---|
| 145001 | *American Jewish Fertility* | Calvin Goldscheider |
| 145003 | *The American Jewish Community* | Calvin Goldscheider |
| 145004 | *The Naturalized Jews of the Grand Duchy of Posen in 1834 and 1835* | Edward David Luft |
| 145005 | *Suburban Communities: The Jewishness of American Reform Jews* | Gerald L. Showstack |
| 145007 | *Ethnic Survival in America* | David Schoem |

Brown Studies in Religion

| | | |
|---|---|---|
| 147001 | *Religious Writings and Religious Systems Volume 1* | Jacob Neusner, et al |
| 147002 | *Religious Writings and Religious Systems Volume 2* | Jacob Neusner, et al |
| 147003 | *Religion and the Social Sciences* | Robert Segal |